# Putting
# Total Quality
# Management
# to Work

# *Putting* Total Quality Management *to Work*

## What TQM Means, How to Use It & How to Sustain It Over the Long Run

Marshall Sashkin & Kenneth J. Kiser

Berrett-Koehler Publishers
San Francisco

**Berrett-Koehler Publishers, Inc.**
155 Montgomery St.
San Francisco, CA 94104-4109

**Ordering Information**
*Orders by individuals and organizations.* Berrett-Koehler publications are available through bookstores or can be ordered direct from the publisher at the Berrett-Koehler address above or by calling (800) 929-2929.

*Quantity sales.* Berrett-Koehler publications are available at special quantity discounts when purchased in bulk by corporations, associations, and others. For details, write to the "Special Sales Department" at the Berrett-Koehler address above or call (415) 288-0260.

*Orders by U.S. trade bookstores and wholesalers.* Please contact Publishers Group West, 4065 Hollis St., Box 8843, Emeryville, CA 94608; tel. (800) 788-3123; fax (510) 658-1834.

*Orders for college textbook/course adoption use.* Please contact Berrett-Koehler Publishers, 155 Montgomery St., San Francisco, CA 94104-4109; tel. (415) 288-0260; fax (415) 362-2512.

**Printed in the United States of America**

Printed on acid-free and recycled paper that meets the strictest state and U.S. guidelines for recycled paper (50 percent recycled waste, including 10 percent postconsumer waste).

---

**Library of Congress Cataloging-in-Publication Data**
Sashkin, Marshall, 1944–
     Putting total quality management to work : what TQM means, how to use it, & how to sustain it over the long run / Marshall Sashkin & Kenneth J. Kiser. — 1st Berrett-Koehler ed.
       p.  cm.
     "Revised and expanded from the original paperback version of this work, entitled Total quality management . . . published in 1991 by Ducochon Press" — T.p. verso.
     Includes bibliographical references and index.
     ISBN 1-881052-23-0 (hardcover: alk. paper) — ISBN 1-881052-24-9 (paperback: alk. paper)
     1. Total quality management.  I. Sashkin, Marshall. 1944–  Total quality management.   II. Title.
     HD62.15.S27    1993                              92-31296
     658.5'62—dc20                                 CIP

---

**First Berrett-Koehler Edition**
Revised and expanded from the original paperback version of this work, entitled *Total Quality Management,* that was published in 1991 by Ducochon Press.

Text design and production: Mary Carman Barbosa
Copyeditor: David Degener
Cover design: Robb Pawlak

# Contents

# Preface

This book started out as a short paper. Both of the authors deal with managers in various educational and consulting situations. Over the past year or two we found an increasing number of managers asking questions or making assertions about *total quality management*. There seemed to be a real need for a brief document that would, in a clear and straightforward manner, describe this concept, answer the most frequently asked questions, and correct the most common misconceptions. So, we started to write an article about that. Before we knew it, our brief article had grown beyond the bounds of a ten- or twenty-page handout. We refocused our efforts on a short monograph. But, again, the monograph got out of hand; we found ourselves with a manuscript that was definitely book-length.

As is always the case in writing, whether a paper or a book, we learned a great deal. Exploring a concept, we sometimes found our initial understanding to be off-target. More often, we saw that our views were incomplete, that a fuller and sometimes significantly more complex perspective was required to really understand what we had thought to be a relatively simple point.

Our first product was a self-published book titled *Total Quality Management*. Several thousand managers, as well as consultants and researchers, read the book; a number of them gave us useful feedback. In general, they appreciated the clear and straightforward writing style. That was good to hear, since we worked hard to make technical complexities clear while avoiding the jargon common to management and behavioral science. But people also told us that they wanted more guidance about what to do to apply TQM. We addressed this need in two ways.

First, we expanded the discussion about implementing TQM in the final chapter. And we added details throughout the book, paying more attention to questions of "how to." Second, we incorporated into the text most of the discussions previously found in the endnotes. Originally, we used these endnotes to deal at length with issues, including application examples, that we thought would interest only scholars or experts who were deeply involved in TQM. However, people kept telling us that some of the best stories and explanations were buried in our notes. In this revision of our book we decided that to the extent possible we would incorporate the endnotes into the text. And we have.

We worried about the length of the revision. But, as it happens, the book is not all that much longer than the first edition. And reviewers of our drafts said that the additions were helpful—and practical. Integrating most of the endnotes into the text seemed to make the book even more application-oriented—thus, our new title, *Putting Total Quality Management to Work*.

We did retain some endnotes (now at the end of each chapter). We didn't do this to engage in side discussions of greater depth that the typical manager might find of little interest. We did it for two reasons. First, the notes enable readers to follow up on ideas of special interest, to locate sources of additional information. Second, we are committed to scholarship. We are both scholars as well as practitioners; our combined university appointments extend for nearly a half century. As scholars we needed these notes because we are committed to full and complete citation of all of the sources of information we use.

It may seem to someone unfamiliar with total quality management that there is considerable agreement among those who research and implement this approach. In fact, there is considerable *disagreement* with respect to approaches to total quality management. One may be a "Juran person," a "Deming acolyte," a "Crosby devotee," or a follower of any of a dozen other "gurus" in the field of total quality management. We have tried to give a relatively balanced treatment of the various personalities involved, but we do have some biases and you will find them easy to identify. Even if we do not seem to follow your own favorite approach, you may still find that we have managed to incorporate the most important elements into our own view.

We received a great deal of help from students, colleagues, and friends. Despite a relatively sound knowledge of the field and its literature, we could never have produced this book without the extensive assistance of many people. To those who made special efforts, we want to express our deepest appreciation and gratitude.

Richard L. Williams prepared the illustrations in Chapters One and Four and in Appendix A, and commented in detail on early drafts of the manuscript. Paul Rossler read and made extensive notes on almost every page of an early draft, often pushing us gently in the right direction. He also designed the control chart we use as an example in Chapter One.

Gregory Boudreaux provided crucial strategic advice, helped us refine and clarify our concepts of how TQM becomes part of organizational operations, and gave many valuable editorial suggestions. He has had a very positive influence on this final product. In terms of both general direction and specific detail, his efforts are visible throughout the book.

Robert M. Fulmer also provided advice of extraordinary quality; he was especially helpful in guiding us to see and improve the flow and organization of the material. Terrence Deal reviewed and responded with specific suggestions to our discussions of culture and culture change. We hope that his deep knowledge of organizational culture and its shaping is reflected in our work. And, by sharing his disagreements, Erich Prien helped us sharpen (and, occasionally, temper) our arguments.

We were fortunate to be able to tap into Paul Tolchinsky's vast knowledge of total quality management in the United States and Japan. Muriel Converse helped us strengthen our descriptions of the TQM culture-building processes described in Chapter Six. Denise Rousseau is a scholar who pressed us to focus on practical applications. Kenneth Blanchard encouraged us both directly and by his leadership model. Finally, we thank Warren Bennis, whose inspiration proved invaluable. His concepts and writings on organizations and leadership are incorporated throughout this book.

We are also grateful to those of our colleagues in organizations who read and reviewed our early drafts, especially CarolAnn Auclair and William H. Clover. Brigette Nix provided extensive and detailed feedback (both her own and her colleagues') on more than one draft. The results of her efforts to get us to address union issues and concerns are evident in Chapter Six and greatly improved the final draft. Special thanks are due Eva Pang, whose master's thesis, "Developing a Quality Improvement Taxonomy," proved to be a treasure trove of definitions, explications, and references. Although we do not quote her work in this book, we recognize our debt to her for doing some of the hardest background work.

Throughout the book we have relied on facts reported in David Halberstam's fascinating book, *The Reckoning*, as well as on Mary Walton's marvelously clear presentation of the ideas of W. Edwards Deming in her book *The Deming Management*

*Method.* To both of these authors we extend our thanks as well as our admiration.

We must also acknowledge the pioneering efforts of those who defined and created the practice of total quality management, especially Walter A. Shewhart, W. Edwards Deming, and Joseph M. Juran. If not for them and those who followed their early lead there would be no TQM to write about.

Finally, for this revision of our original text we were fortunate to have the advice of Bill Schmidt and a second, anonymous, reviewer. Our publisher, Steven Piersanti, has been a source of both concrete advice and encouragement, for which we are grateful. And sincere thanks are due our production editor, Mary Carman Barbosa, for her expertise and patience. Despite our indebtedness to the individuals named above, along with other colleagues whose earlier works form the foundation for our own, this book—and any flaws it may include—is strictly our responsibility, and any blame or errors remain ours alone. Moreover, we do not mean to suggest that the persons named above would necessarily agree with any specific point we make.

Of course, we owe the most (and sometimes give the least) to our families, especially Molly Sashkin, who was deeply involved in the book's design (in both its earlier and present versions) and who coordinated all aspects of its original technical production, and Pamela Peevy-Kiser.

We hope that this book proves useful to you. We are very concerned about the fate of America in the twenty-first century. Like many others who have studied the issues dealt with here, David Halberstam believes, as stated in his book, *The Next Century,* that the post-millennium world will find its center in the Asian nations of the Pacific Rim, not in Washington or any of the (formerly) great industrial cities of the eastern United States. We agree in general with that assessment, but we also believe that it has not yet been decided whether America will share in shaping the twenty-first century or will be forced to live in the past, on remembered achievements. The choice is not a matter of fate or fortune; it is up to us. The ideas in this book are absolutely crucial if we hope to enter the next century as serious players in a "new world order."

*October 1992*

Marshall Sashkin
Seabrook, Maryland

Kenneth J. Kiser
Stillwater, Oklahoma

# The Authors

**Marshall Sashkin** has conducted and applied research on leadership, participation, and organizational change for more than twenty years. For the past ten years his work has focused on top-level leadership. Marshall is the author of the *Leader Behavior Questionnaire (The Visionary Leader)*, used widely in research and executive development. His current consulting assignments include major projects on measuring organizational excellence and changing organizational cultures through leadership. Recent and current clients include General Electric, TRW, the World Bank, and the American Express Company.

Marshall's academic focus has been research in the areas of leadership, participation, and organizational change. He is the author or coauthor of twelve books and monographs and of more than fifty research reports. His work has appeared in the *Psychological Review*, the *Journal of Applied Psychology*, the *Academy of Management Review*, and other research publications. For seven years he served as editor of the research and practice journal *Group & Organization Studies* and, most recently, was assistant editor of the ASTD-sponsored research journal *Human Resource Development Quarterly*.

Marshall grew up in Los Angeles and attended the University of California, Los Angeles, receiving a bachelors degree in psychology. He earned his doctorate in organizational psychology from the University of Michigan. From 1979 to 1984 he was a professor of industrial and organizational psychology at the University of Maryland. As a senior associate in the Office of Educational Research and Improvement, the U.S. Department of Education's research applications arm, Marshall helps develop and guide applied research to improve schools through more effective leadership. He is also an adjunct professor of psychology and administrative sciences at George Washington University and principal partner in Marshall Sashkin & Associates, a consulting firm that provides resources to organizations working toward total quality management. For more information, call (301) 552-9523, or write to MS&A, P.O. Box 620, Seabrook, MD 20703-0620.

**Kenneth J. Kiser** has spent more than a decade working with top-level managers in a wide variety of organizations to improve quality and organizational performance. His current and recent assignments include Virginia Fibre Corporation, Bay State Gas Company, the Naval Ship Systems Engineering Station (Philadelphia), Hillcrest Medical Center (Tulsa), and other small- to mid-sized manufacturing and service organizations. He has practical as well as academic experience, including being a floorman at an open-hearth Bethlehem Steel plant and an hourly employee at a Buick Motors Division parts production supply warehouse. He has been a member of the United Steelworkers Union and of the United Automobile Workers Union.

A native of Oklahoma, Ken earned a bachelor's degree in political science and economics and a master's degree in sociology from Oklahoma State University. He went on to receive his doctorate in sociology from the Ohio State University. The focus of his doctoral study was on systems analysis. From 1985 to 1991 Ken was Associate Director of the Virginia Productivity Center. He was also, from 1988 to 1990, a visiting professor in the Department of Industrial and Systems Engineering at Virginia Polytechnic Institute and State University (Virginia Tech). Ken is currently an associate professor of sociology at Oklahoma State University.

# Introduction

# What Makes
# Total Quality Management Work?

In American business and industry, even in government and public service agencies, the watchword these days is *quality*, often heard as *total quality* or *total quality management*. We will call it TQM, for short. But what *is* TQM, and where did it come from? How does it work? How can an organization adopt a TQM approach? These are some of the questions we will address.

To put it simply, this book looks at three important foundations of TQM. The first concerns tools and techniques that people are trained to use to identify and solve quality problems. The second factor centers on the customer as the focus of TQM. The third factor is the organization's culture. A TQM culture is based on certain values and leadership vision.

In the first chapter we explore the sources of TQM, both people and concepts. We look at what TQM is *not*, in order to contrast what, at its core, it really is. Chapter Two takes up the question of defining total quality management. This is not as easy as it might seem. We focus especially on ideas first expressed by W. Edwards Deming, but we must go beyond Deming to provide a concrete definition (as well as to understand the nature of the "new philosophy of management" that Deming speaks of).

Next, in Chapter Three, we look at the inner workings of TQM, at least those that are most commonly seen and understood. These are the tools and techniques that organization members learn to apply. People are trained to use these tools and techniques to identify and solve quality problems. However, as important as tools, techniques, and training are, they are only the superficial evidence of TQM. Effective implementation of TQM calls for much more than training people to use certain tools and techniques.

In Chapter Four we begin to see what really makes TQM work. What's needed is an all-encompassing determination to meet customer and client needs and deliver quality for the customer. Doing this requires a systemic, organizational application of TQM. We must go well beyond tools and techniques to see how TQM can become an integral part of the organization's operating systems. Even this is not the complete answer; there is still more to TQM.

We turn in Chapter Five to a detailed exploration of the deepest level of TQM: organizational culture and transformation. The new, TQM culture is what supports the driving aim of quality for the customer. To reach this aim, certain values and beliefs must become part of the organization's culture.

These values include, of course, the overriding importance of quality. But the values and beliefs needed to support TQM include much more than a simple belief in the importance of quality. They deal with the nature and definition of what Rensis Likert called "the human organization,"[1] that is, the way people believe they should be treated and the things they value at work. We will examine some value issues of special importance for TQM. These include the basis for rewards, the relationship that should exist between authority and responsibility, and the way people believe they should work together.

Chapter Six explains how to construct organizational cultures that define, support, and sustain TQM, with special attention to the role leaders must play to develop a TQM culture. We also examine the role of unions in TQM. A TQM culture includes everyone and excludes no one. If there is a union then it must be involved in the TQM effort.

In our concluding chapter we outline in some detail how to go about applying TQM. While there are no standard steps, there are some useful guidelines for designing and taking the first steps toward TQM. We also discuss how the issues dealt with in this book are being played out in real-world organizations and what the future might hold for TQM.

In sum, there are three important aspects of TQM:

- *Counting*—tools, techniques, and training in their use for analyzing, understanding, and solving quality problems

- *Customers*—quality for the customer as a driving force and central concern

- *Culture*—shared values and beliefs, expressed by leaders, that define and support quality.

TQM works when people use basic statistical tools and behavioral techniques to count or to collect data in order to analyze and solve problems. People do this not out of an abstract interest in statistics or problem solving. People do it because this is the only way to meet—and exceed—customers' wants and needs. But none of this can happen unless an organization's culture supports it.

If all this seems more difficult than you expected, you're right, it is. But if it seems impossible, then you are wrong. The "impossible" has been done and continues to be done, and not just in Japan. In our review and explanation we will give real examples of American firms, large and small, that have successfully applied

TQM. Only then will it be fair to close with some answers to the question of whether striving for TQM represents a realistic goal.

While our focus is practical, this book is not a step-by-step "how to" guide to TQM. In our final chapter we will outline some important first steps that you can take to begin the process of total quality management in your organization. However, it is important to understand that *there is no generic set of magic steps!* In every case an organization must define its own way. There would be no point in our trying to explain how to implement each of the many specific programs, policies, and actions that could make up a comprehensive approach to TQM. Moving toward TQM is the work of everyone in the organization—leaders and followers, executives and employees. There are, however, many good books and resources to help in applying one or another of these TQM elements. We will identify some of the most useful resources throughout this book, as well as in Appendix C, a brief practical guide at the end.

Our aim is modest. We propose to help you understand what TQM really is, apart from all the hoopla and hurrahs. Then, you can decide whether TQM is right for you. If you conclude that TQM should be part of your own organization, then the first steps to take will be clear and you will also understand—and be able to avoid—the major traps and pitfalls in moving to TQM.

Our own bias is no secret: We believe that unless many more American organizations follow the TQM path, America will enter the new millennium as a second-rate competitor headed downhill. We do not see this as inevitable. There are choices to be made, important ones. Our purpose is to help you make the right choice.

## Endnote

1.    Rensis Likert, *The Human Organization* (New York: McGraw-Hill, 1967).

# 1

# The Roots of TQM

The term *total quality management* means different things to different people. Our aim in this chapter is to arrive at a common understanding of TQM, highlighting those elements or aspects shared by most or all definitions. We begin by examining where TQM came from.

What first caught American managers' attention was a Japanese "import" called *quality circles* (QCs, or quality control circles). The idea behind QCs is to have workers meet occasionally, for an hour or so each week, to discuss work problems. As a result of their discussions the workers develop ideas about how to solve the problems they have identified.

QCs became popular in Japan during the 1960s and '70s. They began formally in 1962, and by 1980 there were over 100,000 QCs in operation in Japanese organizations of all types. Workers would meet in teams around a table at a regular time during the week, usually before or after working hours. The team members would discuss problems, usually concerning the quality of production. Based on these discussions they would develop solutions and pass these ideas on to management. The aim was usually to improve product quality; thus the name, "quality circles."

American firms began using QCs in the mid-1970s; they gained in popularity throughout the 1980s. By 1986 QCs were so common that *Business Week* listed them as a fad of the '80s.[1] The story also noted that QCs seemed to have mixed results. Not every QC installation was a grand success, as the following real-life case demonstrates.

## A QC Installation Example:
## Graft the Leg from the Donkey

In 1980 the management of the admissions office at a large East Coast university decided to start a quality circles program. The 20 admissions office workers were assigned at random to meet in QC groups of four persons each. Since everyone in the office did essentially the same job, random assignment seemed to be the most logical basis for forming groups.

The groups met after work, at lunch, or on break time. As is usual with a QC, the topics were to be work-related concerns and problems, with a view toward possible solutions. While they lacked formal QC training, all employees were college graduates who saw themselves as professionals. These managers apparently felt that their basic group discussion skills were adequate and that no special QC training was needed.

Over the sixteen months during which the QCs operated they discussed many problems but resolved few. After a time, some participants complained to management that the meetings often degenerated into gripe sessions. Moreover, it seemed that those doing the most complaining were interested in doing the least work. Some workers reported that the most frequently discussed problem was how to get away with doing as little work as possible!

After about ten months there were some changes in management; the new managers were much less supportive of or interested in the QC program. When the facts noted above became evident to these new managers, they abolished the program.

Why did this effort fail? Would training have helped the new technique to succeed? Probably not. It is not really hard to understand this failure: The organizational culture in which these employees worked was very different from that of the typical Japanese firm involved with QCs. Instead of a history of loyalty to the organization based on trust and support, there was a history of acrimony and deception. Instead of a shared sense of purpose and problems, there were strong differences in how employees and managers defined both the purposes and problems of the organization.

The employees thought of themselves as professionals. They defined their job as (1) determining whether potential applicants to the university should be admitted, and (2) providing academic counseling for those who were admitted. Despite the employees' college-level training, however, management did not treat them as professionals. Instead, managers saw them as clerks or low-level technical staff. Accordingly, they received much lower wages than did persons with comparable training and experience working in business or industry. And they were subject to controls more commonly applied to hourly than to salaried employees.

While the employees saw themselves as professional admissions counselors, managers saw them as salespersons whose primary task was to market the university to acceptable applicants. The sole criterion for acceptance was the Scholastic Aptitude Test score; anyone scoring above a certain point would be admitted, at least provisionally. Therefore, managers neither expected nor permitted much actual academic advising. Employees were even given pitches to follow when attempting to sign up acceptable potential students.

Our example of the admissions office involved the application of a technique—quality circles—with neither a client-centered purpose nor a systemic organizational commitment to quality improvement. To put it as cynically as some employees felt, management's only real aim was to squeeze more productivity out of employees. Employees who saw the situation this way refused to cooperate; when managers realized this they ended the program.

## The Fading of the Fad

Throughout the 1980s it became obvious that all too many QC "installations" were suffering some variation of the fate just described. In one West Virginia manufacturing plant QCs were installed in 1981 but failed dismally—after the company laid off half its employees.[2]

These and other failures of QCs were probably due more to the way the approach was used than to some flaw with the technique itself. QC trainers commonly offer and provide services to "install" QCs. This treats QCs as something that can be bolted on to an organization, like an afterburner that has been attached to a factory furnace to provide cleaner emissions. W. Edwards Deming, a major force in the movement toward TQM, has said, "A usual stumbling block [in quality improvement efforts] . . . is management's supposition that quality control is something that you install, like . . . a new carpet."[3]

The effect is like trying to graft a donkey's leg onto an overweight cow, to help the cow support her weight. An interesting idea, but sure to be rejected in the end! And probably not without the managers involved getting a few solid kicks of the donkey's leg before it's rejected by the corporate body.

The quality circle technique is best used in the context of an organizationwide quality improvement effort. Used that way, in an organizational culture designed to support TQM, quality circles can be useful and productive. But QCs represent a technique that came later, not a defining attribute of TQM. In Japan the TQM movement started in the late 1940s and was in full swing by 1960. The first QC in Japan, however, was not formed until 1962. It was not until the mid-1970s that QCs were widespread in Japan—and being introduced (or re-introduced) in the United States.

## QCs: The "Made in America" Import

If QCs had been a Japanese invention, designed to suit the Japanese organizational culture, it would be understandable that their implementation in American organizations might be problematic. The technique, however, was not really new. It was in the 1940s that American industrial consultants—in a men's shirt and pajama factory—first got groups of workers to talk over and try to solve their everyday work problems.[4] Some of the consultants' associates went on to apply this technique in other organizations. A variety of American organizations used this group problem-solving approach over the next 25 years.

For example, at Detroit Edison in the late 1940s Norman R. F. Maier, an American industrial psychologist, introduced an employee team problem-solving approach very similar to the QC concept. In one instance a crew assigned to clean coal-fired furnaces redesigned their work process, to the initial opposition of engineers who had designed it as a four-day job and who believed that a worker-designed alternative would take much longer. The crew's new plan cut the furnace down-time from four to two days, a 100% improvement. The new plan was far more satisfactory to the crew members themselves. And the effect was not short-lived; it held up over time.[5]

Despite a variety of similar successes, the approach that inspired Japanese managers to invent quality circles did not become popular in the United States until, after a quarter century, it was reintroduced as an "exotic" Japanese management technique!

Is there evidence that quality circles really work, that they really improve production quality? The answer must be a *qualified* yes. That is, QCs typically start out heralded as a major new quality improvement approach, and they often appear to deliver results, at least at first. But after the initial enthusiasm fades it often becomes clear that nothing has really changed. Eventually, both workers and managers lose interest in QCs. In many organizations QCs just fade away within a year or two.

After QC failures such as the one detailed above, consultants as well as managers realized that for QCs to take root and make a long-term difference, more would be needed than a room with a table and chairs and an hour a week overtime pay for the workers. It was about this time that American management discovered *quality improvement* (which has now become so popular that it has all but replaced earlier attention to *productivity improvement*).

This discovery came in two stages. First, American consumers began to turn to Japanese, not American, manufacturers for quality products. That's one reason for the fad-like initial popularity of QCs—managers thought, "Maybe this is the Japanese 'secret'!" However, people eventually realized that whatever the merit of QCs, they were not the secret behind Japan's success.

In looking more closely at the why and how of Japanese quality, American managers stumbled across a more important part of the "secret:" an *American* industrial consultant, W. Edwards Deming. He first gained widespread attention in the early 1980s, after being featured in an NBC television documentary titled "If Japan Can, Why Can't We?"[6]

## The Remarkable Dr. Deming

W. Edwards Deming began his career as an industrial engineer investigating problems of quality control. Working at the Hawthorne plant of AT&T's subsidiary firm, Western Electric, Deming observed the production of switching equipment and other telephone-related hardware.

Curiously, it was in this same plant, toward the end of the 1920s and into the 1930s, that the now-famous "Hawthorne Studies" were conducted. These experiments provided the first formal research on the effects of human relations in organizations. As research experiments, the Hawthorne Studies were flawed in very basic and important respects. Even so, they provided the first opportunity for formal, real-life study of the effects of physical and social conditions, including supervisory style and employee participation.[7]

Although Deming was not involved in the Hawthorne Studies, his experiences in the Hawthorne plant impressed on him the need for basic changes in how employees were treated. He concluded, in particular, that piecework—the system of paying a worker for only the number of complete, acceptable items that a person produces—was one of the most demeaning and dehumanizing work systems ever invented. Says Deming, "Piecework is man's lowest degradation."[8]

Piecework puts great emphasis on identifying defects and requires constant and comprehensive inspection. But Deming realized that the traditional practice of inspecting all products and sorting out those with defects, to be corrected later, was both foolish and costly. He pointed out that quality is not improved by after-the-fact inspection but by control over the production process as it happens. Deming saw that workers were the only parties who could, and had to, exercise such control. The problem was that the typical worker had neither the latitude nor the skills needed to do so.

In the early 1920s Western Electric created a new department, to study the problem of quality and its control. Deming learned firsthand of the groundbreaking work of a key member of this group, an engineer named Walter A. Shewhart. Shewhart was the first to recognize the importance of understanding and measuring the *variability* of a product's dimensions and attributes. Then one can seek out the causes of variations beyond acceptable limits. Finally, one can take actions and make changes to reduce variability or bring it to within the acceptable range.[9] Shewhart devised statistical techniques for making these types of measurements. He also invented ways to display the results in easy-to-follow graphs.

After receiving a doctorate in physics from Yale, Deming accepted a position with the U.S. Department of Agriculture. He continued to study with Shewhart, who was then leading a research group at Bell Labs in New Jersey. In the 1930s and '40s, working with Shewhart and on his own, Deming refined and improved on Shewhart's ideas and tools. He modified Shewhart's specification-production-inspection cycle of quality control activity, inventing what is now known as the Deming Cycle (plan-do-check-act).[10] He even improved some statistical methods first developed by Shewhart, publishing his results as papers and reports in various professional journals.

Deming also spent a great deal of time teaching others to use the quality control tools and techniques he had learned, modified, or invented. Deming taught engineers, technicians, and ordinary employees how to make project timeline charts (or *Gantt charts*). He showed them how to take random samples of output and then plot the variability of important characteristics on *statistical control charts*.

## Controlling Variability

The single tool most associated with Deming and his statistical process control approach is the *control chart* (see Figure 1). A control chart is a graphic display of measurements of an important product or process variable. In a manufacturing situation an example might be the diameter of a ball bearing. In a service context, the measure might be the presence or absence

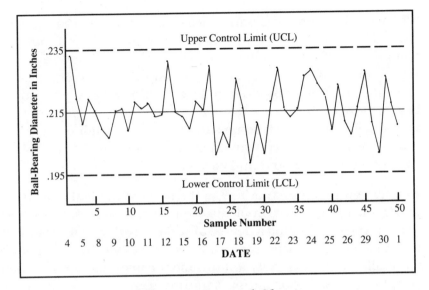

**Figure 1: Control Chart**

on an insurance claim form of certain required information. The measure is taken at different times, using a statistical sampling procedure. The control chart displays these results over time. The chart is designed on the basis of a normal distribution, that is, the classic bell-shaped curve. This chart makes it easy to see whether the actual measures fall within the statistically defined limits of such a distribution.

The upper limit is called the "upper control limit," abbreviated UCL, and the lower limit is called the "lower control limit," or LCL. When measures on the control chart are above the UCL or below the LCL, the process is out of control. Through careful study one must find out what is wrong, what is varying in a nonrandom manner. Is the steel rod used to make ball bearings too hard? Too soft? Is the cutting adjustment on the rod cutting machine set incorrectly? Does the machine not maintain the setting? Is the timer on the grinding/smoothing machine that rounds the ball bearings not running consistently? Or, are employees leaving the machine on too long (or not long enough)?

When a distribution of product measures is normal, that is, bell-shaped, it is safe to assume that there are no unknown outside factors that affect variability in consistent ways. If there are, the distribution will appear tilted or skewed in one way or another. If the distribution of product or service measures, such as ball-bearing size or the time it takes to respond to a service request, is not bell-shaped, or if some sample measures fall outside the limits shown on the control chart, the cause of the undesired variation must be found and corrected.

Neither control charts nor any of the other statistical tools used in TQM actually solve problems. The control chart tells us that something is producing a degree of variability that is undesirable and unacceptable. Control charts can also identify when such variability occurs. Quality improvement comes about only when people use this information to study a problem, identify its causes, determine how to correct it, and take action.

One usually isn't satisfied just to have the variability fall within the UCL and LCL. Generally, the measurement tolerances allowed for a product or service—the specifications—will be tighter than just plus or minus three standard deviations. The maximum desired measure will be below the UCL and the lowest acceptable measure will be above the LCL. Once a process is in control, one looks not just for samples above the UCL or below the LCL, but for samples that fall outside the specification limits.

But constant improvement of quality does not simply mean staying within certain limits. The work process must be studied and improved so that variability is constantly reduced. This is the only way to consistently reach a specific, desired product or service measure and thus increase the level of quality.

The issue at the heart of quality control is understanding and controlling the variability in key or crucial aspects of a product or service. The steel from which ball bearings are made must be neither too soft nor too hard. The machines that cut the steel wire into small bits must not cut bits that are too big or too small. The smoothing and grinding machine that makes the ball bearings perfectly round must not run too long (and make bearings too small) or not long enough (leaving bearings rough and irregular).

The first task is to find out whether variation is random or whether there is some specific source that is causing consistent, undesired variation from the average. Then, when the sources of such problems are identified, actions are designed to remove that variability. The goal is to control variability so that it is due to truly random variation and not to defective materials, maladjusted machinery, or incorrectly designed production operations. Next, the work process is studied and changes are made, so that variation is kept within certain, specified limits. Finally, one works to narrow those limits, to reduce variability further and further.

The purpose of all of the statistical tools associated with TQM is simply to obtain measures that will help determine ways to control and reduce variability. Control charts, like all of these tools, are really just structured ways of counting and displaying the results. The tools of statistical process control have at least three important uses. First, they help to describe and understand a work activity, or *process*. This is a matter of counting, recording, and interpreting the results. Second, tools help people to identify, focus on, understand, and correct the causes of abnormal variation. Third, these statistical tools provide the information that's needed to figure out how to change and improve work processes, so that higher levels of quality can be achieved. This is what continuous improvement is about, in terms of statistical process control.

## Sources of Variation

We have given some examples of possible causes of undesired variation, but there are two important categories of causes. The cause of variability might be something done, not done, or done incorrectly by a worker. Deming refers to these as *special causes*. However (and, according to Deming, far more likely), the cause might instead be due to problems with raw materials, the manufacturing process, or the service plan. These problem sources are attributable to, and are the responsibility of, management, not workers. Deming calls them *common causes*. No matter how motivated workers may be to do a good job, problems caused by the system—common causes—cannot be corrected by telling employees to try harder, by rewarding them for better results, or even by punishing them for undesirable outcomes.

Managers typically assume that problems (like too many oversized ball bearings) are caused by employees' actions. Deming believes, however, that such assumptions are usually wrong, that the real causes are often beyond employees' control. Deming argues that the underlying causes of most quality problems are the responsibility of management, especially top management, not employees.

Management designed and maintains in operation the systems that cause the problems. When a work process is out of control due to bad raw materials or machinery defects, workers cannot be blamed for the poor quality of the output. Nor do they generally have the authority to take action to correct the problem.

According to Deming, only about 6% of all problems are due to special causes, including employee error or failure to perform. The other 94% are, in his judgment, caused by systems—work processes, procedures, and machines—that are out of control and, as designed, not easily controllable. Because top management designed and put these systems in place, the problems they cause are management's responsibility.

The exact numbers Deming uses to express the proportion of quality problems due to common and special causes have varied over time. Others put the proportions of common to special causes at 85% to 15%. As best we can determine, Deming's and anyone else's figures result from personal guesses, not empirically determined facts. There do not appear to have been any formal experiments to see whether Deming's estimate is correct.

We believe that the 15% figure is about right. People are usually hired for jobs on the basis of either demonstrated skills or after testing to make sure that they can perform the job effectively. Once on the job, most organizations provide employees with training to improve their job performance. These two factors, selection and training, are very likely to reduce the extent to which problems are due to employee error.

It may still be true, as some argue, that employee performance accounts for a much larger proportion of problems than Deming suggests. It may account for 20%, 30%, or as much as 40% of work production and performance problems (although we doubt that it is anywhere near this high). However, this does not change the fact that some proportion, and probably a fairly large proportion, of problems are due to work processes and systems that are out of statistical process control. Current approaches to management typically ignore such problem causes. This makes it impossible to correct many quality and performance problems. In contrast, TQM deals with problems of both types. This is much more important than knowing exactly how much of the overall problem is due to employee error and how much to other common and special causes.

## Training People to Apply Statistical Tools: The Answer?

Control charts, quality control circles, and all the other tools and techniques we will describe have the same aim: helping people to track and then control variability in manufacturing or service processes.[11] It might, then, seem that training people to use these tools will lead to TQM. Many organizations have taken just this approach.

In the mid-1980s a small manufacturer in the Midwest that supplied parts to the auto industry decided to apply statistical process control (SPC) techniques throughout the organization to improve quality. Working with a local college and with some special support from a state job-skills development program, human resources department staff developed and implemented a plan for training all employees in SPC.

First, top managers attended an introductory seminar. Next, technical, supervisory, and managerial employees went through a series of short training sessions to learn how to use the basic tools, including control charts. The technical personnel received additional training in applying some more sophisticated tools to solve quality problems. Finally, a group of internal trainers learned how to teach employees and managers to use the basic SPC tools, to train new employees, and to give others refresher courses.

The training program ended after about four months and, for a time, the results seemed positive. During the second year, however, there was less use of the tools, both by lower-level employees on the line and by the more technically qualified staff. Managers, especially at the top, became less and less involved in the ongoing SPC program. Top-management support, which from the start of the project was more a matter of encouragement than active involvement, became less evident.

Today, there are still individuals in this firm who use one or another of the basic tools. Many of the more senior technical personnel report that they sometimes use certain advanced tools. However, there is nothing that could be called a coherent program, focused on quality control or quality improvement.

This firm's experience has been repeated often. A company acts on its commitment to training, people learn to apply various tools and techniques, and everything looks great—for a while. But then the use of tools and techniques drops off; people go back to the old ways or just don't bother to go to the trouble of making and maintaining control charts. Why, we must ask, does this happen?

## Why Do Tools Fail?

Our example, though it happened in the 1980s, merely repeats Deming's experience of almost a half-century earlier. That is, during the 1930s and '40s Deming's teachings (in addition to Shewhart's ideas and those of other quality control consultants) were widely adopted by American industry. Deming found himself training group after group of workers, supervisors, and engineers in his quality control methods.

In the 1940s, Deming took a new assignment with the federal government, applying his methods to national measurement problems, focusing on industrial production for the war effort. Again, he had many successes. Chronicling the decline of the American automobile industry in his book *The Reckoning*, David Halberstam points out how during the war Japanese engineers would examine captured American military equipment and marvel at its quality. It was then that they first realized, according to Halberstam, just how hopelessly outmatched they were.

After the war, when Deming returned to industrial consulting in American organizations, he was surprised to find no one using his methods; hardly anyone even remembered them! For a while, he tried to teach the methods to a new generation of workers and engineers, but his efforts had little lasting impact. The workers and engineers were interested, but their managers didn't seem to care.

American management was riding the postwar boom, with an undemanding and apparently inexhaustible supply of consumers who wanted products, after years of wartime scarcity. Quality did not seem to be important to them. Deming realized that despite all his work before the war, he had made no lasting impression on the organizations he had worked with because he had made no impression on management. He took a position with the Bureau of the Census, as a statistical sampling expert.

## If Not America, Why Not Japan?

In the late 1940s the Bureau of the Census sent Deming to Japan to help the postwar Japanese government improve its census-taking capability. Deming made contact with industrial engineers, too. In 1950, still generally ignored by American industry, he returned to Japan at the invitation of a new professional organization of engineers and scientists.

The founders of this organization, the Japan Union of Scientists and Engineers (JUSE), were concerned about the very poor quality of Japanese products. They intended to change this situation. Deming agreed to help with a lecture tour, talking to large groups of technicians, researchers, engineers, and plant managers.

In her book *The Deming Management Method*, Mary Walton reports that in the middle of his first lecture Deming had a sense of déjà vu. He realized that if he simply lectured and taught his methods to engineers and technicians, the same thing that happened in the United States would happen in Japan. That is, when consumer demand grew, management would abandon his methods and focus on production at the expense of quality.

This realization led Deming to see if he could get to the "right people," the top executives of Japanese organizations. Ichiro Ishikawa, a member of the committee that had invited Deming, was a former professor of many such top executives. Ishikawa was also head of Keidanren, the Japanese Federation of Economic Organizations, Japan's most prestigious and powerful organization of business leaders. Deming knew nothing of this; he simply asked his host, Ishikawa, whether it might be possible to arrange a special session with a group of top industrial managers.

In *The Reckoning*, Halberstam tells how Ishikawa cabled top Japanese industrial leaders, inviting them to attend Deming's lecture. Coming from Ishikawa, the invitation had the effect of an order; every one of them showed up. Two more meetings with almost a hundred other top managers followed—all in addition to the lectures that Deming gave for thousands of technical personnel.

Unlike American managers, Japanese top managers paid attention to Deming. They went to work with a passion; they knew they had to rebuild their industrial base if Japan was to prosper in the coming years. They were well aware of Japan's reputation for inferior quality. To become a real competitor in the world economy, Japan had to change and improve.

The Japanese executives applied Deming's lessons rigorously throughout their organizations; they truly took Deming's teachings to heart. At first, some—perhaps many—doubted that Deming's methods would work. They applied them anyway, to avoid losing face by disobeying this American expert, sent by the U.S. government to help them.[12]

Throughout the 1950s Japanese firms vied among themselves to see which could go the farthest in applying Deming's ideas. They quickly established an all-industry competition and an annual prize for the organization that demonstrated the most comprehensive and effective applications. Teachers are honored and respected in Japan, so they named the prize after their first and most important teacher, W. Edwards Deming.[13]

Deming was a good student as well as a teacher. One of his former students at New York University, Rafael Aguayo, observes that Deming "believes every student has something to offer, something to teach. Deming goes to a class or seminar prepared to learn as well as to teach."[14] He learned from his disappointing post-war experiences that simply teaching people to use statistical tools aimed at quality improvement was not enough. Only management produced quality. He later observed that "no permanent impact has ever been accomplished in quality control without [the] understanding and nurture of top management."[15]

The Japanese proved that Deming had learned the right lesson. They went far beyond applying this or that tool; they invented or adopted many new tools—some much more sophisticated than Deming's. But they never lost sight of the end, the aim, the purpose for using the tool. That purpose was to produce the level of quality of goods and services that customers wanted.

## Was It Deming or Was It Japan?

Deming was not the only American consultant to go teach the Japanese about how to improve their manufacturing base. He was not even the only one to receive the Order of the Sacred Treasure (Second Rank) from the Emperor; he shares that honor with another well-known quality consultant, Dr. Joseph M. Juran.

Juran first went to Japan several years after Deming, and he made the same sort of lecture/consulting tours. Many years later, Juran was asked whether it was true that he and Deming had been the key forces behind Japan's post-war turnaround. Some people in the West, Juran replied, think

> the Japanese miracle was . . . due to two Americans, Deming and Juran, who lectured to the Japanese soon after World War II. Deming will have to speak for himself. As for Juran, I am agreeably flattered but I regard the conclusion as ludicrous. I did indeed lecture in Japan as reported, and I did bring something new to them—a structured approach to quality. I also did the same thing for a great many other countries, yet none of these attained the results achieved by the Japanese. So who performed the miracle?[16]

In *The Reckoning* Halberstam emphasizes Deming's role. Even so, he observes that right after the war (and before Deming appeared) there was a small group of key Japanese industrial leaders who had already concluded that Japanese manufacturers had to change radically if Japan was to aspire again to industrial greatness. They recognized that this change had to emphasize productivity *and* quality. Some of these men were the very ones who had laboriously translated the early work of Shewhart into Japanese—and who had invited Deming and other quality consultants to come to Japan to teach them about quality improvement.

One of the prime movers in this group was Dr. Ichiro Ishikawa, a founder of JUSE, an early chairman of Keidanren—the most powerful association of top business leaders in Japan—and a professor at Tokyo University (Todai), the elite college in Japan from which future industrial leaders invariably graduate. Ishikawa was a crucial member of the group of Japanese industrialists who helped foster Japan's industrial recovery through quality. His son, Kaoru, followed in his father's footsteps, becoming a senior official of JUSE. Kaoru Ishikawa also founded the JUSE Quality Control Research Group and wrote several important books on quality control and TQM, including a popular book that has been translated into English.[17]

There is an even more basic—and less obvious—factor that helped Japanese companies to focus quickly and successfully on the aim of customer and client quality satisfaction. This factor comes into play because Japanese organizations are far more homogenous and cohesive than firms in many other countries. The cultural cohesiveness and strength characteristic of Japanese organizations reflect the cultural homogeneity of Japanese society. Visitors who have been in Japan for any length of time know the experience of being treated as *gaijin*—outsiders. There is little room in the Japanese culture for outsiders; at best, one is politely tolerated. At worst, one is openly ostracized.

In developing a societal commitment to rebuilding their industry on the basis of quality and customer satisfaction, the Japanese had the advantage of a strong social culture. In developing an organizational commitment to quality, Japanese firms started with a similar advantage due to strong and cohesive *organizational* cultures.

The observations of Halberstam and of Juran lead to the same conclusion. That is, in Japan it was possible for top-level industrial leaders to consciously decide to pursue quality with the greatest possible effort and to do so consistently, across industries. Shortly after the war, MITI, the powerful Ministry of International Trade and Industry, made this aim explicit.

Certainly Deming, Juran, and a few others (including Ichiro Ishikawa and his son, Kaoru) were key players in the dramatic revitalization of Japanese industry. But to suggest that they were the primary cause would be missing the point. TQM depends not on consultants or techniques but on making the strongest possible commitment to quality improvement.

## But What *Is* TQM?

In this chapter we have identified the origins of TQM. It may have surprised you to discover that the crucial elements of TQM identified so far all seem to have American, not Japanese, origins. We've spent the most time on the essential core of TQM practice: measuring, controlling, and reducing variability. But we have not yet discussed the why or the dynamics of how TQM is achieved. As stated in the Introduction, there are three fundamental aspects of TQM: *counting, customers,* and *culture.* Customers represent the "why," culture the dynamic "how" of TQM. We will discuss each, in detail, in later chapters. First, however, we must complete our definition of TQM.

## Endnotes

1. "Business Fads: What's In—And Out," *Business Week*, January 20, 1986, p. 60.

2. See the work cited in note 1.

3. W. Edwards Deming, "Report to Management," *Quality Progress*, July 1972, p. 2.

4. Lester Coch and John R. P. French, Jr., "Overcoming Resistance to Change," *Human Relations*, November 1948, pp. 512–533.

5. See Maier's book, *Problem Solving Discussions and Conferences* (New York: McGraw-Hill, 1966), for more details on work-group problem solving.

6. "If Japan Can . . . Why Can't We?" Narrated by Lloyd Dobyns. Broadcast by NBC on June 24, 1980.

7. For more information on the Hawthorne Studies, see the classic book *Management and the Worker* (Cambridge, MA: Harvard University Press, 1939), by the Harvard researcher whose name is most closely associated with this work, Fritz Roethlisberger, and his internal organizational counterpart, William H. Dickson.

8. Mary Walton, *The Deming Management Method* (New York: Putnam/Perigee, 1986).

9. Shewhart's book *The Economic Control of Quality of Manufactured Products* (New York: D. van Nostrand, 1931), is still in use. It is the classic work in the field of statistical process control.

10. In his latest writing Deming has changed the term "check" to "study."

11. We will discuss statistical tools in more depth in Chapter Three and describe some in more detail in Appendix A.

12. The most interesting account of how Deming came to help shape the nature of Japanese industry is told in David Halberstam's book *The Reckoning* (New York: Morrow, 1986). The book tells the story

of the decline of the American automotive industry and corre-sponding rise of Japanese automakers. Halberstam's account differs somewhat from that given by Mary Walton in her book *The Deming Management Method* (New York: Putnam/Perigee, 1986), considered by many as the definitive "bible" of the Deming approach.

13.  Deming also donated the royalties from his books, which had become very popular in Japan, to fund the prize. There are two major Deming Prize categories, one for organizations and one for the individual who best exemplifies application of quality methods. New categories have recently been established for organizations that have previously won the Deming Prize, and for foreign organizations.

The Malcolm Baldrige National Quality Award is sponsored by the U.S. Department of Commerce. In many ways it emulates the Deming Prize. Candidates submit extensive applications, docu-menting how they meet each of seven major criteria designed to assess how well an organization has succeeded at total quality management. The criteria used for the Baldrige Award are consis-tent with and similar to the characteristics of TQM that we define in this book. More details on the Baldrige Award can be found in Appendix B.

14.  Rafael Aguayo, *Dr. Deming: The American Who Taught the Japanese About Quality* (New York: Carol Publishing Group, 1990, p. xiii).

15.  W. Edwards Deming, "Report to Management," *Quality Progress,* July 1972, p. 2.

16.  Joseph M. Juran, "Product Quality: A Prescription for the West, Part II: Upper-Management Leadership and Employee Relations," *Management Review,* July 1981, p. 61. Quoted in David A. Garvin, *Managing Quality* (New York: Free Press, 1988, p. 184).

17.  Kaoru Ishikawa, *What Is Total Quality Control? The Japanese Way* (Englewood Cliffs, NJ: Prentice-Hall, 1985).

# 2

# What Is TQM?

We can now see that TQM is not quality circles, statistical process control, or any of the other tools developed and taught by Deming and others. Such tools are necessary because they enable people to carry out the activities that produce quality, but the tools are not TQM. To understand the basic nature of total quality management, we must take into account the two other aspects mentioned earlier: customers and culture.

Consider first a Japanese technical definition of quality control. Japanese Industrial Standard Z8101-1981[1] states that quality control is

> a system of means to economically produce goods or services
> which satisfy customers' requirements.

This standard goes beyond the notion of tools to incorporate a more sophisticated understanding of TQM. This new concept has two parts. First, it refers to "a system of means." That is, the tools are just part of the means, and they are used systematically, as a coherent and integrated approach. Second, this definition centers on the pervasive and persistent focus on customers and what they want. This simple standard makes it clear that quality is much more than a collection of tools and techniques, that it includes a focus on customers and on a system that has certain characteristics.

But Japanese Industrial Standard Z8101-1981 still does not give us a complete definition of TQM. Yes, TQM does incorporate a very strong focus on customers and a coherent, integrated approach to quality, but that is neither an adequate definition nor an accurate explanation for the success of Japanese firms in using TQM.

To understand why, we must go further for a definition of TQM. We must look again at the ideas of W. Edwards Deming.

## Deming Again

We return, one more time, to the ideas about quality expressed by W. Edwards Deming. We do so because, unlike many other quality experts who remained focused on tools, techniques, and training, Deming became less concerned with these factors over time. Increasingly, Deming concentrated on TQM as a culture or, as he calls it, a *philosophy of management.*

Deming once was asked by a magazine interviewer why the Japanese had applied his teachings so successfully when American managers had not. In response, Deming said, "I think there is something fundamentally different [between Japanese and American business managers]. The best description I can think of is that the people have roots, and the roots are the company."[2]

In the forty years between 1950 and 1990, Deming began to focus increasingly on his realization that management mattered even more than tools. He came to speak somewhat less about control charts, although he never stopped teaching people how to use these and other tools. He began, however, to talk more about *management* and about the *philosophy* that management must develop and implement to achieve quality.[3] This new way of thinking is at the heart of his famous fourteen points, and of his seven deadly diseases that afflict American management.

At different times, Deming has referred to the points as *principles* or as *obligations*. The number, too, has increased over the years. When we turn to the fourteen points, we quickly leave techno-jargon behind in favor of the management of culture. Consider Deming's points:[4]

1. **Create constancy of purpose for improvement of product and service.** Not only does Deming stress the need for a continuing emphasis on quality improvement, he also, more subtly, points out that quality, not profit, should be the primary purpose. Profit, for Deming, is a consequence, a by-product, of a management approach centered on quality.

2. **Adopt the new philosophy.** Here Deming reiterates the need for constancy of purpose while emphasizing how important it is for this purpose to be shared by everyone in the organization and inculcated like a philosophy, which it really is.

3. **Cease dependence on mass inspection.** Quality cannot be added on; it must be built in from the start. Mass inspection is completely off the mark. It assumes that quality can be achieved by identifying and then correcting errors. As Walton observes, this means that workers are paid to make errors and are then paid again to correct them. This is not to say that workers like this any more than do managers. Deming notes that almost all workers want to do work of high quality, work in which they can feel pride and a sense of accomplishment.

4. **End the practice of awarding business on price tag alone.** Deming does not advocate ignoring price when looking for suppliers. He only insists that price is a relatively minor factor, especially compared with the supplier's interest in and

willingness to meet the customer's needs—that is, the needs of the organization that purchases the supplies. (Those needs, of course, are driven in turn by the needs of the organization's clients and customers.) Choice among suppliers should be based mostly on the quality of the materials they supply and on their willingness to work to improve that quality in the context of a long-term relationship.

Wal-Mart was known for years for its tough negotiating style with suppliers. But several years ago, CEO Sam Walton decided that poor relations with suppliers were hurting the company. He changed the strategy to one of working with suppliers to develop new products that customers wanted and to improve the quality of production and delivery processes. In 1990, Wal-Mart passed Sears as the nation's largest retailer.[5]

5.  **Improve constantly and forever the system of production and service.** This point restates management's never-ending obligation to seek out ways to improve quality. An interesting story is told by one member of a team from an electronic controls manufacturer formed to visit Motorola and study its exceptional system of production quality. A Motorola vice-president showed the team a pager that was selling well on the Japanese market. He explained that the product had a mean time between failures (MTBF) of 100 years and that Motorola was working to extend this to 125 years. One visitor said to the vice-president, "Excuse me, but isn't that just a little extreme? After all, who would see a problem with an MTBF of 100 years?" The vice-president gave the questioner a steely glare and said, "Constant improvement is what we are all about."[6]

6.  **Institute training.** Deming does not limit training to the use of statistical quality control and other tools for improving quality. He also means training in how to do the job. Many workers never get adequate training in doing the jobs for

which they are responsible. In American industry, about 70% of all training dollars go for management education and development. Only 30% is spent on training for lower-level line employees, those who actually make products or deliver services. This imbalance can not only lead to errors, it makes it more difficult for workers to figure out what management expects of them. In Japan, the proportions of funds spent on training for workers and training for managers are approximately the reverse. To make TQM work, front-line employees must receive ongoing training.

7. **Institute leadership.** Being a leader is different from being a supervisor. Supervisors tell workers what to do and then watch to make sure they do it. They administer rewards and discipline as needed to ensure that employees comply with orders. In contrast, leaders assume that workers want to do the best job they can. At lower organizational levels, the job of a leader is to assist workers by coaching and by arranging for training when needed. For top management, leadership means designing the system on the basis of TQM, applying strategic vision to build a TQM culture, and constantly and consistently modeling behavior that exemplifies the values that support such a culture.

8. **Drive out fear.** This is without a doubt one of the most important of Deming's points. In many organizations, people are afraid to speak up, to point out problems, or just to ask questions. Managers rule by fear, using either special favors or, more often, various punishments to make sure that workers do as they are told. People are sometimes fired for bringing a problem to the attention of management. A concern for quality requires that employees feel secure. High quality cannot be attained unless managers operate in a culture of openness, in which no one is afraid that telling the truth, pointing out a problem, or trying to learn to do the job better will lead to the loss of one's job.

9. **Break down barriers between staff areas.** Traditional organizational structures encourage competition among units, departments, divisions, and so on. But this makes it difficult, if not impossible, to work together to achieve quality. People in different areas and departments must understand that they have the same overriding goals, that they are in competition with other organizations, not with their colleagues and coworkers.

10. **Eliminate slogans, exhortations, and targets for the work force.** In this point, Deming is criticizing those who think that quality can come from motivation, from getting people all worked up through motivational speakers and inspirational tracts. This approach actually makes things worse in the long run, because even if workers really want to do better they still don't know how, they don't have the tools they need to improve, and they are not supported by the organization's culture. Deming has said that slogans and targets put people in the position of having an idea of where they want to go but no map of how to get there.

11. **Eliminate numerical quotas.** Quotas encourage people to ignore quality. The goal is to meet or exceed the quota at any cost and regardless of quality. Even when quality meets specifications, quotas can have hidden costs. For example, one department may produce its quota, but the products, while technically meeting specifications, may not meet the needs of the department's internal customer, another department that uses the output of the first as one important part of a larger product. The result will be continuing conflicts as well as the added costs of rework so that the first department's output is fit for use by the second department, its internal customer. Mary Walton notes that inefficiency and high cost are also common outcomes when numerical quotas are stressed. Goals must focus on quality issues, not on numbers produced.

12. **Remove barriers to pride of workmanship.** Eliminate the annual rating or merit system. Deming assumes that people want to do a good job, not a poor one. They need help in overcoming such barriers as the poor quality of the materials they receive to work with, the poor quality of their equipment, and inadequate job training. It does not help when people feel that they are being judged, ranked, and rated. A management-designed and supported system of operation is needed that allows all employees to do their jobs well, not one that tries to coerce performance from them.

13. **Institute a vigorous program of education and improvement.** Deming does not downplay the need for everyone to have a thorough grounding in the tools and techniques of quality control. These tools are the language of quality. But he also points out that people must learn new ways of working together as teams and new behaviors that support the new management philosophy—the TQM culture.

14. **Take action to accomplish the transformation.** Everyone in the organization must work together to implement a quality culture. Top management in particular must focus on a strategy and a plan and take actions to put the plan into effect. Workers cannot be expected to do it on their own, no matter how much training they receive in the use of quality control tools and techniques. Only management can begin the process of getting the entire organization—management as well as workers—to take the actions that result in a TQM culture.

These fourteen points are the basic elements of Deming's new philosophy, his operational theory of management. Only when these elements become an integral part of the organization's culture is TQM in full operation. It would be foolish to state or suggest that Deming's fourteen points are the only possible basis for TQM, that nothing else is needed or useful, or that all fourteen points are equally important. But it is equally foolish to think that one can pick and choose among the fourteen, using only those one likes.

This is often what happens when top executives hear Deming or read about his approach and decide to begin a TQM program. In such cases, they often focus on the points that deal with training in the use of statistical tools. The more fundamental but more difficult to implement points, such as *drive out fear* and *eliminate numerical quotas*, are ignored. The results are the type of TQM failures described in Chapter One.

Deming is under no illusion about the difficulty of bringing a new way of thinking to American organizations. To do so, he asserts, means overcoming what he labels the *seven deadly diseases:*

- Lack of constancy of purpose to improve products and services by providing resources for long-range planning, for research, and for training

- An emphasis on short-term profits and the quarterly dividend

- Individual performance evaluations through merit ratings and annual reviews

- Managers who are highly mobile and hop from company to company

- Use by management of numbers and figures that are visible and available with no thought of the information that may be needed but unknown or hidden

- Excessive medical costs

- Excessive legal liability costs, which can be swelled by lawyers who work on contingency fees.[7]

Some of these "diseases" are restatements in negative form of one or another of the fourteen points. Nonetheless, except for the last two items, all these "sins" of management refer to beliefs, policies, and practices so firmly entrenched that many, perhaps most, American managers regard them as basic truths.

For example, managers in American organizations typically assume that every employee has his or her own goals and that each department or division has its own aims. A common view is that it is only natural that these various parties compete to get what each wants. Managers presume that this will be best for the organization. But this is rarely the actual outcome. Much more often, competition within the organization over multiple goals leads to conflicts and hard feelings. The compromises that typically result neither satisfy the parties nor benefit the organization. These conditions are what Deming refers to when he speaks of a lack of constancy of purpose.

Most American firms also accept the proposition that they "need" to satisfy stockholders with high dividends every quarter. The resulting focus on short-term profits, on quarterly stock dividends, and on driving up the value of the company's stock is so pervasive that two Harvard Business School professors have pointed to this notion as responsible in large part for what they call "managing our way to economic decline."[8]

The pervasive acceptance of individual performance evaluations puts an inappropriate and dysfunctional emphasis on competition and on placing one's own interests above those of the organization as a whole. It also encourages the wrong use of data, that is, to judge results and control people (and by controlling people improving results). The effective use of data involves understanding and improving the operations that produce these results.

In a *Wall Street Journal* interview, Deming said, "We rank people with incentive pay, annual appraisals . . . [but] judging people is not helpful . . . Ever heard of a bank that closed? Do you think it closed because of sluggishness and errors, mistakes at the tellers' windows, mistakes in bank statements, mistakes in calculation of interest? Don't be silly. It closed because management made bad loans. That's from incentive pay and ranking people. A bank lending officer has a quota to lend $83 million per month. He does it, and can you blame him? That was his job. Other lending officers do the same. And the bank gets into trouble."[9]

Americans are now so mobile that we sometimes forget that it was not always this way. Deming observed that Americans put entirely too much emphasis on the lifetime job guarantee that some (by no means all) Japanese companies give their workers. He points out that we do not emphasize enough that most Japanese companies give this sort of guarantee to their *managers*. This removes the need for job-hopping and increases the chances that managers will be committed to the organization and its purpose.

Finally, Deming notes that American managers often have massive compilations of data at their fingertips. Just as often, however, these data are useless for controlling or improving quality. That is, we try to use the information that we happen to have or know how to get without even asking why or for what purpose we need that information. "Costly computers turning out volumes of records is not quality control," says Deming.[10] Only by asking the right questions can one figure out what sort of data, what numbers, what figures are necessary.[11]

## Why Deming?

It may seem that we have concentrated overmuch on Deming and, worse, been uncritically favorable toward his ideas. Moreover, for all his contributions, Deming is also known as a classic curmudgeon, so set in his views that he cannot conceive of other possibilities. And he is a colorful speaker, often embarrassing his hosts with comments not just blunt but profane!

While Deming's breadth of vision has, in some ways, proved exceptional, there have been many others who have made important contributions to the development of TQM. The roster of "founders" would, for example, include Ichiro Ishikawa and his son Kaoru Ishikawa,[12] Joseph M. Juran, and Armand V. Feigenbaum, who coined the term "total quality control."[13] In Chapter Four we present a model of the TQM process that derives, in part, from the work of D. Scott Sink and his associates at the Virginia Productivity Center.[14] Chapter Five explores in depth the nature of TQM cultures; we cite the work of Tom Peters (of *In Search of Excellence* fame),[15] Joe Scanlon (who developed one of the earliest gainsharing plans),[16] and the Dutch psychologist Geert Hofstede (who studied organizational cultures in forty different nations).[17] Many people—Japanese, Americans, and Europeans— have had a hand in creating and developing TQM. Some, of course, have made contributions of special significance.

In Chapter One, we mentioned the contributions of Kaoru Ishikawa, son of Ichiro Ishikawa, the early Keidanren leader who helped Japanese executives identify the need for quality and who invited Deming to teach Japanese business executives how to achieve quality. Kaoru Ishikawa is best known in Japan and in the United States for his efforts to develop and spread the use of TQM tools and techniques. Not only has Ishikawa written several technical yet clear books that describe TQM tools and explain how to use them, he has also developed new tools, such as the *fishbone diagram*. This simple chart, which resembles a fish skeleton, helps people to focus on and specify possible causes of problems. It is often referred to as an *Ishikawa diagram*.[18] Kaoru Ishikawa's contributions to TQM, especially with respect to the tools needed for effective application of TQM, have been very great. We will have more to say about tools in Chapter Three and Appendix A.

Another TQM guru whose work has been of major significance is Dr. Joseph M. Juran,[19] a contemporary of Deming's. Juran, too, worked in the Western Electric/Bell Laboratories group founded by Shewhart, and he also lectured to the Japanese on quality a few years after Deming's lecture to Keidanren leaders. Juran established an organization to carry out his ideas, The Juran Institute, which delivers public and in-house seminars on quality around the world. Juran's greatest contribution has been in defining and teaching how to create customer-oriented organizational systems. In such systems, a concern about quality for the customer is built into all organizational operations. In Chapter Four, we will draw on the work of Juran and others that deals with the organizational focus on quality for the customer.

Finally, although we speak little of Deming in Chapter Five, that chapter is largely an attempt to apply what we know about organizational culture to make Deming's TQM philosophy of management more specific and concrete.

In this book and especially in this and the preceding chapter, we do focus a lot on Deming. We do so not because he is the best known or the most colorful of the quality gurus, although he is both. Our reason is simple: Deming's approach comes closer than any other to identifying the cultural issues that define and drive, support and sustain TQM. Tools are necessary but not sufficient. A concern about quality for the customer that pervades every organizational operation is imperative but inadequate. Only when top management makes a real commitment to creating a TQM culture is there the slightest hope that TQM will be attained.

In the course of his long and productive career, Deming found that the very fabric of organizational life, the organization's culture, must define and support TQM. Deming's approach is really an approach to management, a prescription for building the sort of culture that will support TQM. By defining positive aims and by identifying the negative barriers that must be overcome, Deming offers management a comprehensive system for achieving TQM. His system starts with but goes far beyond statistical process control and the other tools and techniques that have come to be incorrectly identified as TQM. The ideas expressed in Deming's new philosophy of management are at the heart of TQM.

## A Definition

The ideas presented in this chapter help us to go beyond tools and techniques, even beyond the ways in which a customer focus must be built into organization operations, to understand the cultural basis of TQM. With this in mind, we can finally define total quality management:

> *TQM means that the organization's culture is defined by and supports the constant attainment of customer satisfaction through an integrated system of tools, techniques, and training. This involves the continuous improvement of organizational processes, resulting in high quality products and services.*

For TQM to work, certain tools will be needed, tools that most American organizations use poorly if at all. For TQM to succeed, management must believe in and act to achieve quality for customers and clients as a primary organizational aim. But the underlying essence of TQM, the existence and definition of TQM, is using tools to achieve the aim of quality for customers by creating a *culture*, a pattern of shared values and beliefs. Culture supports the aim of quality for the customer and encourages the commitment of *all* organization members to that end. Before we explore TQM culture in detail, however, we will look at how it works—through tools—and then at how it centers on the customer.

## Endnotes

1.  Another of the many formal and informal cultural supports designed to enhance the quality of Japanese products, the powerful Ministry of International Trade and Industry (MITI) first developed and now enforces a set of uniform standards for industry called the Japan Industrial Standard (JIS). There are many organizations in the United States that have developed product standards and codes—mostly voluntary (like Underwriters Laboratory, which certifies that electrical products meet defined safety standards). While obtaining the JIS imprint is not technically a legal requirement in Japan, the culture-based value of meeting the standard is so strong that most organizations operate as though the standards had the force of law. Japanese manufacturers would not even consider not undergoing the rigorous review and enforcement procedures defined and overseen by MITI.

2.  This quotation is taken from an interview, "Dr. W. Edwards Deming—The Statistical Control of Quality: Part I," *Quality*, February 1980.

3.  Deming's ideas are presented clearly by Mary Walton in *The Deming Management Method* (New York: Putnam/Perigee, 1986). A more sophisticated and elaborate presentation can be found in *Dr. Deming: The American Who Taught the Japanese About Quality* (New York: Carol Publishing Group, 1990) by Rafael Aguayo. To read Deming's own words, see his book *Out of the Crisis* (Cambridge: Center for Advanced Engineering Study, Massachusetts Institute of Technology, 1986).

    Only in very recent years have many American organizations become interested in Deming's ideas. More and more, however, have started to ask how to attain high quality so as to regain their competitive advantage. Thus, in his nineties, Deming continues to maintain an active schedule of seminars and consulting assignments that would tax the energies of a person half his age.

4.  The titles of the points are, for the most part, the same as in Deming's book *Out of the Crisis*, while the definitions are based both on Deming's most recent writing and on our interpretation of the descriptions that Mary Walton presents in her book The *Deming Management Method.*

5.   Thomas C. Hayes, "Behind Wal-Mart's Surge, a Web of Suppliers."
     *New York Times*, July 1, 1991, pp. C1, C2.

6.   K. Hawley, *Executive Quality Management—What You Get Is What
     You Lead* (Minneapolis, MN: Undersea Systems Division, Honeywell
     Corporation, 1989).

7.   Our descriptions of the seven deadly diseases are based on those
     given by Mary Walton in *The Deming Management Method.*

8.   They also blame another of Deming's deadly diseases, the mobile
     manager who is, in their words, "a pseudo-professional" who can
     supposedly jump from one top-level job to another without any
     hands-on knowledge or experience of the organization's core
     production technology or more than the most simple understand-
     ing of complex organizational issues. See Robert H. Hayes and
     William J. Abernathy, "Managing Our Way To Economic Decline,"
     *Harvard Business Review*, July/August 1980, pp. 67–77.

9.   Interview with W. Edwards Deming, *Wall Street Journal*, June 1,
     1990.

10.  W. Edwards Deming, "Report to Management," *Quality Progress*,
     July 1972, p. 41.

11.  Based on comments in "Dr. W. Edwards Deming—The Statistical
     Control of Quality: Part II," *Quality*, March 1980.

12.  Even some TQM experts have confused the two Ishikawas. The
     father, Ichiro, was a founder of the Japan Union of Scientists and
     Engineers (JUSE) and a leader of the influential association of top
     business leaders, the Keidanren. Ichiro Ishikawa recognized the
     need for quality early, helped to translate Shewhart's classic book
     on statistical control, and invited Deming to meet with elite business
     executives to convince them of the need for quality. The son, Kaoru,
     was also a leader in JUSE, although his focus was on teaching
     people to use statistical tools and techniques to improve quality. He
     even invented one, the cause-and-effect diagram, also known as the
     *fishbone diagram* or the *Ishikawa diagram.*

13.  Feigenbaum was the first to use the term *total quality control,*
     meaning essentially what we now call TQM, in his classic article
     "Total Quality Control," *Harvard Business Review*, November/

December 1956. He expanded on this in his book *Total Quality Control* (New York: McGraw-Hill, 1961).

14.    D. Scott Sink and Thomas C. Tuttle, *Planning and Measurement in Your Organization of the Future* (Norcross, GA: Industrial Engineering and Management Press, 1989). Sink and Tuttle's work draws on and extends earlier systems approaches defined by Deming.

15.    Tom Peters, *Thriving on Chaos: Handbook for a Management Revolution*. New York: Knopf, 1988.

16.    Frederick G. Lesieur (Ed.), *The Scanlon Plan: A Frontier in Labor-Management Cooperation* (New York: Wiley, 1958).

17.    Geert Hofstede, "Motivation, Leadership, and Organization: Do American Theories Apply Abroad?" *Organization Dynamics*, Summer 1980, pp. 42–62.

18.    The Ishikawa diagram is explained in more detail in Appendix A. Kaoru Ishikawa's best-known English-language book is *What Is Total Quality Control? The Japanese Way* (Englewood Cliffs, NJ: Prentice-Hall, 1985).

19.    Juran has written many books, but the most important is probably his *Quality Control Handbook* (New York: McGraw-Hill, 1951). The most recent edition is called *Juran's Quality Control Handbook* (New York: McGraw-Hill, 1988). A current book by Juran and Frank M. Gryna, Jr., is *Quality Planning and Analysis from Product Development Through Use* (New York: McGraw-Hill, 1989).

# 3

# TQM Tools and Techniques

In a way, it is easier to explain how TQM works than it is to define what it is. That is, TQM works because of the organization's culture, through the organization's structure and management processes, and by means of various tools and techniques that employees learn to use. It may sound too simple, but it's still true that TQM is based mostly on rational thinking and problem solving. However, to enable people to think and act rationally and creatively, organizations require complex, nontraditional cultures.

Deming has observed that plant managers in America often start the day with reams of computer-generated statistics. While these data may spell out in detail all the plant's quality problems, they usually tell the manager nothing at all about how to correct the problems. Simple, rational thinking could, however, lead to a short report that, in Deming's words, "would tell [the manager] that at ten o'clock yesterday morning something went wrong on the line. At the same time, a new supplier's material went into use; the reason for the problem is a characteristic of the new material . . . . Too many companies," Deming concludes, "try to get along by using hardware instead of brains."[1]

The use of tools and techniques is the most visible evidence of TQM. It is, however, also the most superficial indicator of TQM and cannot be relied on as such. Statistical tools alone cannot lead to quality or TQM. Group problem-solving techniques like brainstorming or the nominal group technique may help teams solve specific work problems, but they will not lead to TQM, even when every team has been trained to use them. The respected American quality consultant Joseph M. Juran has said that "a good way to lose time in improving quality is to focus on tools and try to apply them."[2]

Juran's approach to quality, like Deming's, involves the use of a number of tools. But, again like Deming, Juran recognizes that while they are necessary and useful, tools alone cannot lead to TQM. The most basic and general tools are brainpower and rational thinking. This is, perhaps, expressed most clearly in the Plan-Do-Check-Act (PDCA) cycle, a technique made popular by Deming (that he attributes to his mentor Walter Shewhart; Deming always calls it the *Shewhart cycle*).

The four steps in the cycle involve exactly what they state. First, *plan* carefully what is to be done. Next, *do* it, that is, carry out the plan. Third, *check* the results. Did the plan work as intended, or were the outcomes different, perhaps even undesirable? Finally, *act* on the results, both positive and negative. This means identifying what worked as planned and what did not, then taking these results into account to develop an improved plan and start a new PDCA cycle. The four-step PDCA sequence is really nothing more than a straightforward rational problem-solving process.[3]

## The Seven Old Tools

Rational problem solving is what Deming had in mind when he said that organizations need more brains, not more machines.

Admiral Grace Hopper, who helped design the first computer and develop the first computer language, observed that when we organize raw data—the "facts"—we produce information. But information, Admiral Hopper went on to say, is not worth much until the brain processes it and turns that information into *intelligence.*

Computers and management information systems (MIS) do a wonderful job of turning data into information, producing massive automated reports on demand. However, only the human mind can make sense of what is happening to cause problems. To do this, people do not usually need huge stacks of computer printout. What they do need is carefully designed, timely, and accurate counts presented in straightforward ways. Even more important is thinking through what one *wants* to happen and figuring out how to *make* it happen. In this sense, problems arise when something doesn't work as we planned or expected.

The jargon of quality control, SPC, and TQM includes the so-called seven old tools. The term *old* is used to set them apart from various "new" statistical tools. These new tools are much more sophisticated and complex than the old ones, but, while they can be very useful indeed, they are not really required for TQM. In fact, the seven old tools are far more important, because *all* tools are really just procedures for counting, that is, for collecting and presenting data. There are only two requirements. First, the data must show clearly when things are not working as planned or expected. Second, the presentation should make it as easy as possible to identify the underlying causes. The seven old tools are useful for identifying both common and special causes of work process problems.

The same can be said about various TQM techniques, such as team-based practices for using TQM tools to solve problems and improve quality. In Chapter One we saw how one especially useful technique, team problem-solving discussions called *quality control circles*, can backfire. This happens when techniques (or tools) are thought of as a complete quality program. Tools and techniques work only when they are applied in the context of a TQM approach designed to create the sort of culture needed to support TQM and to build concern over quality for the customer into all organizational operations.

*What are the seven old tools?* We have provided brief descriptions and illustrations of the seven old tools in Appendix A, rather than in this chapter. We did this for a reason. Our purpose here is not to focus on tools at all but to point out that, all too often, tools and techniques become the focus of all TQM-related activities. When this happens, as we showed in Chapter One, the TQM effort is almost sure to fail. Our point is not that tools are unimportant, only that they can prevent people from seeing and dealing with the far more important elements of TQM: customers and culture.

Our descriptions of the seven old tools in Appendix A are very brief, even sketchy. Perhaps the clearest step-by-step explanations can be found in Kaoru Ishikawa's classic book, *What Is Total Quality Control?*[4] Both study and hands-on practice are needed to master each of these tools. That is precisely what Deming insists on when he advises that management must provide on-the-job training along with "a vigorous program of education and self-improvement" for all employees.[5]

Most of the seven old tools have been used for many years, some since the mid-1800s. Like the quality circle technique, it is not the tools themselves that are really new. Rather, it is their *use* as an integral part of TQM. The tools are just ways to display information visually, ways that help those responsible for quality and performance see how a system or process is operating. People can then interpret the information to identify problems. They can look for causes and take a rational approach to solving the problems that are identified.

## New Tools

There are many other tools that we could describe. The Japanese have been especially effective, not only in developing ways to teach people to use TQM tools but also in inventing new tools. Some that were developed by one or another TQM guru, such as the design-of-experiments approach developed by Genichi Taguchi (often called *DOE* or the *Taguchi method*) have become quite popular. At the same time, various TQM tool experts engage in disputes about whose methods are best. For example, Keki Bhote, the chief technical TQM expert at Motorola and a disciple of another TQM guru, Dorian Shainin, argues that Shainin has conclusively shown that Taguchi's approach is flawed, while Shainin's similar method is technically far superior.[6]

There is also a set of seven new tools, including such tools as fault tree diagrams, affinity diagrams, and factor analysis.[7] Many of these new tools involve sophisticated statistical analysis techniques. Some new tools are more likely to be used by engineers than by work groups. Even so, many of the new tools can be and are being used by lower-level employees to improve quality.

Refinements of the tools and techniques described here, along with other new TQM methods, are common in Japanese organizations. For example, Matsushita Electric Works in Hakone uses a seven-step technique called *total production maintenance* (TPM).[8] First, the machine operators learn to clean their machines using standard cleaning procedures. (In this and many similar industrial operations, each worker identifies closely and personally with the machine. Many machines have pictures of operators displayed on their sides, often with inscriptions like "I love this machine."[9])

In the second step, once employees master the basic cleaning procedures, they learn to adjust the machine when something goes wrong. The third step involves a more complex and thorough grounding in cleaning and oiling. Fourth, the worker becomes responsible for total inspection of the machine operation, using the manual. Fifth is total inspection followed by preventive maintenance. Sixth is understanding of product quality as it relates to the operation of every detail of the machine. At the seventh and highest level, the operator alone becomes responsible for total preventive maintenance. It takes three years, on the average, for an operator to become qualified at the fifth level.[10]

Another Japanese organization uses a different version of TPM called *the five S's* (sometimes also called *the four S's plus S*). This is because in Japanese the words *cleaning (seiri), tidiness or arrangement (seiton), sweeping/washing (seiso),* and *cleanliness (seiketsu)* all start with S. The fifth S stands for the Japanese word for *discipline (shitsuke).* This is a more general concept compared to the other four S's, each of which represents a very concrete activity related to maintaining the physical plant.

Many books are now available that describe one or another of the basic or advanced TQM tools and techniques, often in great detail. Japanese organizations constantly invent new TQM program elements, such as the two just described. Part of the TQM philosophy is that there must be continual improvement. To stick with current technology is to go backward. This applies both to tools and techniques for quality control and to the production or service technology of the organization.

Despite these continued advances, one must always keep in mind that the *tools* and *techniques* are not TQM. Not even training every employee how to use these tools and techniques will implement TQM effectively. TQM operates only when the value of quality for customers is an important part of the organization's culture.

## The True Importance of Tools

A look at popular approaches to TQM might give the wrong impression about the real importance of tools and techniques.

It would probably suggest that TQM consists largely of introductory seminars for upper-level managers focusing on awareness followed by training seminars for lower-level personnel in which they learn how to apply various tools and use certain techniques. Such approaches to TQM are almost certain to fail. The key to TQM is not having everyone learn to use certain tools and techniques. It is the development of a whole new system of management and operation. Nevertheless, in certain respects, tools and techniques are very important for this new approach.

The importance of TQM tools is often diminished by the way in which they are taught: to large groups, by rote, with examples that don't relate well to trainees' actual work. Tools should focus on and be learned in the context of their real uses, that is, as applied to the real work needs of trainees. Thus, a strategic analysis group needs real skill in flowcharting, while a sales team may require less emphasis on that tool but much more on the use of Pareto charts. But this is really just common sense. All teaching should begin with the needs of the learners, not the needs of the teachers. By matching needs, the right tools permit the learner to solve problems and improve work processes.

The deeper importance of tools, however, is that they teach two important but subtle lessons. First, they teach the meaning of variability, which is at the technical heart of TQM. Using TQM to strive for continuous improvement requires people to understand the causes of problems: uncontrolled variation. Second, by learning to use TQM tools, people learn to control variability, and control of variation is the technical means to TQM. This is not a simple or obvious point. The use of TQM tools to analyze and control variability means that random change no longer needs to apply, that people can come to understand work processes and then go on to control and improve them.

While these points are obvious from a practical angle, they have deeper implications. Their real importance is psychological. That is, being able to control one's work and work outcomes through the use of TQM tools shows people that they can be *causes*, that they can control and determine how things turn out. This contrasts with the all-too-frequent role of the worker as a passive, ineffectual bystander, unable to achieve the sort of results expected and of which he or she is capable.

When tools are used effectively, they create in users a sense of what psychologists call *self-efficacy* or what ordinary people refer to as *self-confidence* and *self-esteem*. These attitudes don't come, as some seem to think, from motivational pep talks or from being told how wonderful and valuable one is. Self-confidence and self-esteem result from doing and succeeding, from recognizing that success was due to one's own actions, not to fate or chance.

Thus, TQM tools selected and targeted to the needs and types of problems that users face don't just teach about variation. And they do more than just provide users with the means to solve problems of uncontrolled variation. TQM tools teach users that they can control their own work outcomes. They create in users a sense of self-control that is a crucial prerequisite for long-term success.

Like tools, TQM techniques have an important, less obvious purpose than simply providing structured ways for people to work together more effectively to solve quality problems. Techniques like quality circles and group brainstorming help people develop the skills needed for effective teamwork. They reinforce the team structure that is usually a crucial aspect of the sort of organizational culture that supports TQM. Other techniques, like quality function deployment or design for manufacture (both described in the next chapter) emphasize cross-team cooperation and the systems viewpoint, two important aspects of the culture that supports TQM.

In sum, tools and techniques, the most obvious operational aspects of TQM, are useful from a practical viewpoint. TQM tools help people to collect and analyze data so they can solve quality problems and make continuous improvements. TQM techniques facilitate group problem solving. But the deeper importance of TQM tools is to enable people to develop a sense of control over their own work and work outputs. And the real importance of TQM techniques is their effect in facilitating team operation and cooperation between units.

## The Tools Are Not TQM

People often confuse TQM with tools like those described here, with techniques such as quality control circles, or with training activities that teach employees to use tools and techniques. But tools, techniques, and training are not TQM. To confuse tools with TQM is like saying that great literature is good grammar. Of course, without knowing how to read, write, and construct a clear sentence, one is not likely to produce a great novel. But knowing how to do these things no more guarantees one a literature prize than knowing how to use tools ensures success in TQM.

Tools, techniques, and training are merely the most visible, superficial aspects of TQM. Tools are necessary but not sufficient for TQM. When made the focus of TQM, through training, tools and techniques can even prevent the organization from taking the additional steps needed for TQM. In this way an over-emphasis on tools, in the mistaken belief that the tools are TQM, can lead the organization in the opposite direction, away from an organizational commitment to quality.

In recent years, many organizations have adopted one or more of the tools and techniques just described, often at great cost. Typically they dropped them not long afterward (or they maintain them only in a ritualistic, practically meaningless form). This happens when the underlying TQM value—the overriding importance of quality for the customer—is neither recognized nor part of the organization's culture.

This is what Deming discovered after World War II. Despite his success in training workers and engineers throughout the United States to use his tools and techniques, his efforts, for the most part, came to nothing because management had not adopted the philosophy that the tools and techniques were intended to support. According to Halberstam, Deming continued for a time to train young engineers, but, as Deming later put it, "I was lighting a lot of fires, but they were all going out."[11] His observations and discussions with managers and others helped Deming figure out why. He concluded that it was the lack of management interest and support that led organizations to abandon his earlier teachings and that dissipated the effects of his efforts after the war.

Fortunately for the Japanese, Deming recognized this and, as detailed earlier, focused on gaining the commitment of Japanese top managers. And it would be wrong to fail to mention that, in recent years, some American executives and corporations have also made that commitment. While the number is small, it should not be neglected.

But to what exactly is this commitment? Is it to the abstract ideal of quality? We think not. Quality is what the commitment is *about*, but it is not the whole of the issue. The great German sociologist Max Weber said that to understand anything that happens in a social system—a group or an organization or a society—one must examine the way in which means relate to ends. Tools and techniques are the means, not the ends, of TQM. To fully understand TQM, we must ask about the ends to which these tools are turned: Quality for what? Before turning to the key elements of the new philosophy, that is, to the culture of TQM, we must first answer this very basic question.

## Endnotes

1.    Interview, "Dr. W. Edwards Deming—The Statistical Control of Quality: Part II," *Quality*, March 1980.

2.    Quoted in "Talking Business With Juran of the Juran Institute: Value of Quality to U.S. Managers," *New York Times*, February 6, 1990, p. D2.

3.    See Marshall Sashkin and William C. Morris, *Phases of Integrated Problem Solving* (King of Prussia, PA: Organization Design and Devel-opment, 1985).

4.    Kaoru Ishikawa, *What Is Total Quality Control? The Japanese Way* (Englewood Cliffs, NJ: Prentice-Hall, 1985).

5.    This is one of Deming's fourteen points. See Mary Walton, *The Deming Management Method* (New York: Putnam/Perigee, 1986).

6.    Keki R. Bhote, *World Class Quality* (New York: AMACOM, 1991). Bhote rates the gurus, saying

> Phil Crosby is the showman, useful for companies in the dark ages of quality. Juran is superb for general quality management. Deming now concentrates on twisting top management's tail. Shainin alone is the consummate "tool" man . . . a portly man . . . worth his weight in both gold and diamonds . . . .

7.    Michael Brassard, *The Memory Jogger Plus* (Methuen, MA: GOAL/QPC, 1989).

8.    Seiichi Nakajima, *Introduction to TPM* (Cambridge, MA: Productivity Press, 1989).

9.    If this seems uniquely Japanese and culturally inapplicable to the United States, see William T. Morris's book *Work and Your Future: Living Poorer, Working Harder* (Reston, VA: Reston Publishing, 1975); see especially Chapter Three, pp. 96–99. Morris gives examples involving American workers in U.S. organizations and suggests that a surprising number of Americans have strong emotional attachments to the machines they work with.

10.     Japanese organizations favor long-term job security for pragmatic, not altruistic, reasons. One such reason is to make sure that training investments, such as total production maintenance training, are not lost when laid-off workers take jobs with competitors.

11.     David Halberstam, *The Reckoning* (New York: Morrow, 1986, p. 315).

# 4

# Quality for the Customer

The various tools mentioned and described in Chapter Three and Appendix A all aim to improve the quality of a product or service. This means studying and improving organizational processes, especially how products are made or services delivered. But it can be easy to forget that TQM is not a search for quality as some sort of holy grail or high-tech ideal.

General Motors (GM) recently developed a new high-technology heads-up display (HUD) that flashes dashboard data (fuel, speed, and so on) on the windshield. Drivers can see the information without taking their eyes off the road. However, despite the relatively low cost there have been few takers. Only about 6000 of almost 600,000 potential buyers have ordered the device, for a sale rate of just over 1%. A GM official said, "We gave people whiz-bang technology that they did not want, did not value and weren't ready to use."[1]

The reason to be concerned with quality is that quality is the customer's concern. Juran addresses this issue when he says, "Quality is fitness for use."[2] Thus, Juran recognizes that it is the user who is really the concern, not some abstract ideal of quality. Deming, too, links quality to the customer when he states that by quality he means "economic manufacture of product that meets the demands of the market."[3] According to Deming, it is market demand—that is, the customer—that defines quality. Armand Feigenbaum is even more direct when he observes, "Quality is what the customer says it is."[4]

This means that management must actively reach out to identify and understand the needs and desires of customers. The effort must be continual, since customers' needs and desires change over time. The successful family-owned department store, Nordstrom, maintains such an orientation. Nordstrom is quite profitable, and its salespeople earn among the highest wages in the industry, all despite relatively high prices. The key is commitment to the customer. Nordstrom's CEO recently said, "All of us in the generation now at the top started out as shoe salesmen, serving the customer by sitting at his or her feet and fitting shoes."[5]

The basic importance of a concern about quality for the customer can be seen if we compare two very successful East Coast food markets: Stew Leonard's dairy store in Norwalk, Connecticut, and Wegmans Food Markets in upstate New York.[6] In an article in Nation's Business, Michael Barrier shows that while the two organizations have very different market strategies, they share an exceptionally strong concern over quality for the customer.[7]

Stew Leonard and Danny Wegman have visited each other's stores. Neither is overly impressed. Leonard ridicules the 57 types of mustard that Wegman has on the shelves; Stew Leonard's carries just two. Danny Wegman retorts, "We're not subscribers to niche marketing . . . Stew wants you to shop elsewhere, so you'll . . . appreciate what he's doing . . . We don't want you to have to go anywhere else for anything you need."[8]

But neither niche marketing like Leonard's that concentrates on superb quality and service with a limited line nor full service that provides every possible item variety customers might desire is the answer. What *both* stores  do is concentrate on what customers want and provide it at the highest level of quality. Tom Leonard searches for customer complaints, not compliments. He says, "I thank them so much for calling, because I can go out and solve the problem right now." Stew Leonard, Jr., runs a focus group discussion with a dozen randomly selected customers once a month to get ideas for improvement.[9]

Wegmans not only makes sure that customers get the variety they want, it concentrates on being part of the communities that it serves. Wegmans uses focus groups, too, but it also has a scholarship program for kids who bag groceries (there are more than 17,000 employees, in all). And Wegmans made a conscious decision not to build superstores, in order to stay close to customers at the local, store level.[10]

Both Leonard's and Wegmans invest heavily in employee job training, and both have profit-sharing plans. Both promote from within—and not just family, though both are family owned. All three Wegmans vice-presidents have spent their work lives in the company, starting as teenage baggers.[11] Although the two firms look very different and appear to have different operating strategies, a closer look shows that they are quite similar: Both are driven by the desire to provide quality for their customers.

## The Drive for Quality

Some American organizations have gone beyond a focus on the tools of TQM to focus on quality for the customer. It has become less rare to hear that an organization aims for quality and customer satisfaction above all else. One even finds evidence of such goals in organizational practices. And employees are often well aware of the need for quality for the customer. But what is the source of such a drive for quality? Although it is a positive indicator, a concern for the customer and quality is not always a sign of effective TQM. Often the reason is a simple business value: maintaining market share and profitability.

A concern for the bottom line is not a bad reason to examine TQM. However, it is not enough to establish and maintain a TQM culture. Concern for profit alone cannot sustain TQM over the long run. The *real* issue is concern for the customer through quality. When quality for the customer is the bottom line, then other things will follow, including profit.

Just asserting one's concern with quality for the customer is not enough. To succeed, TQM must be grounded in the organization's culture. Slogans and superficial trappings cannot create or support a TQM culture. They may even contribute to the failure of TQM efforts. Deming warns against signs and slogans. He says, "Exhortations and platitudes are not effective instruments of improvement."[12] Popular slogans are created and repeated without a concern for ways of attaining the aims they promote. This is, says Deming, like goals without plans or destinations without maps—useless. Eventually, people become tired and give up.

What happens when management makes quality for the customer a driving value? People throughout the organization use some, perhaps many, TQM tools and techniques. Moreover, employees receive training in how to apply the tools and techniques to their work.

A closer look proves even more interesting. One often finds that the application of TQM tools and techniques in organizations that make concern for the customer a driving value is not limited to the manufacturing, production, or direct customer service areas. Instead, there is a coordinated and integrated effort to apply TQM. This effort centers on what have come to be called *quality checkpoints.* There are five primary quality checkpoints; we will examine each one.

## The Five Quality Checkpoints

Think of manufacturing or service delivery as the flow of a stream. Suppliers and vendors provide various materials (which can be information as well as physical). These raw materials then move through production points and work processes that transform them into outputs—finished products or services. These outputs then go out the door and are delivered to clients and customers. There are, then, five specific points at which quality can be checked.

First and most important, quality can be identified by whether and how well a product or service meets customers' needs and desires when in actual use. This is the first quality checkpoint. Far more common, quality is checked by final inspection of the product or service on completion. Final inspection prior to customer delivery or use is the second quality checkpoint. The third checkpoint involves the actual production or service delivery process. Statistical process control and many of the other tools discussed in Chapter Two and Appendix A were designed to assess quality in the process of production or service delivery.

The quality of the raw materials that are transformed into a product or service can be examined and assessed when the materials are delivered by suppliers and vendors. This is quality checkpoint four. Finally, one can go to the suppliers and examine how they produce the materials they provide, to assess the quality control they exercise. This is quality checkpoint five. We will examine each checkpoint to discuss what is and should be done.

### Quality Checkpoint 1

It might seem logical to refer to the first step in the manufacturing or service planning process—obtaining materials from suppliers—as the first quality checkpoint (QC1). Instead we look to the customer. Both Deming and Juran point out that customers are even more important than the production process itself. Only when one knows what the customer needs, wants, and expects can one design production processes that will meet those desires. Then, of course, the organization must ensure that the production process is in control, but that comes *after* finding out what customers want, not before. Because TQM begins with the customer, that is where we locate QC1. Continuously, obtaining accurate and timely information about the needs, wants, and expectations of customers is the top priority and the driving force of any TQM system.

Activities at QC1 include customer surveys, focus group sessions with clients, and open-ended customer interviews. (Recall that both Stew Leonard's and Wegmans use focus group sessions to gather customers' ideas and understand their needs.) When feasible, it is appropriate to include customers in product planning, engineering, and problem-solving meetings. At QC1, an organization that's serious about TQM will use a variety of methods to learn what customers need, want, and expect, as well as when and how customers' desires change.

Despite an increased focus on listening to the "voice of the customer" (a phrase that has come into vogue), some organizations have stubbornly maintained old habits. In designing the Chevrolet Caprice, for example, GM's chief of design got feedback from customer panels. These potential customers uniformly agreed that the Caprice design was one of the ugliest cars they had seen in years. One frequent suggestion was to modify the rear wheel wells, to make the car look just a bit more sporty. The design chief rejected even that minor advice. He said, "customers don't know beans about what they're going to like . . . That's the designer's job." General Motors has lost hundreds of millions of dollars on the Caprice; sales are less than half what had been projected. Few individuals actually bought the car; most are sold to fleet buyers—police, rental firms, and taxi companies. Analysts think that GM actually loses money on each car sold this way because of the heavy discounts.

Harvey Mackay, best-selling author and CEO of a Minneapolis envelope manufacturing firm, developed a 66-item questionnaire that is used to learn as much as possible about each customer. The questionnaire is not sent to customers. Instead, it is referred to and updated by employees whenever they contact a customer, to add more information about the customer to the company's file. By learning as much as possible about its customers, the highly successful Mackay Envelope Company is able to respond to their needs better than its competitors.[13]

## Quality Checkpoint 2

QC2 is the point at which products leave the organization. For services, it is the point of final planning prior to service delivery. QC2 has historically been the primary focus of so-called quality control activities: Check to see that the car runs properly and that all systems function as they should before shipping it for sale. Check to see that the rugs are now as clean as standards require. Conduct a test to show that the copying machine now produces perfect duplicates.

The tendency of management to emphasize this checkpoint to the detriment of others led Deming to assert as one of his fourteen points, "Cease dependence on mass inspection to achieve quality!" Final inspection is far less important than some other quality checkpoints, because quality must be designed and built into the product or service. It cannot be "inspected in" later. Still, many organizations expend disproportionate resources and attention on QC2, and many so-called quality control departments are merely inspection units.

This is not to suggest that final inspection is unnecessary. It will always be important to make sure that defective products are not through some accident sent out to customers. Under TQM, final inspection is accomplished using statistical sampling techniques, not by inspecting every item. When final inspection information is channelled properly, it may even be useful for quality improvement. But when TQM is actually practiced as part of an organization's culture, the organization really does cease to *depend* on final inspection to ensure quality. Quality has been designed and built into the product or service.

## Quality Checkpoint 3

QC3 is located at the site of production or work activity. It is the focus of many of the tools and techniques developed for quality control. The control chart is one of the most common tools used at QC3. While statistical process control (SPC) was developed for use in manufacturing, statistical tools are now used in service organizations, too. (Actually, it was in the 1940s that Deming showed how SPC could be applied to clerical work.)

An emphasis on QC3 is desirable, but many organizations, in a rush to apply TQM, overdo it. They fall into the trap of trying to improve *all* the many elements that make up the production process. Instead, they should concentrate on the few *critical* elements that are of the greatest importance for quality.

Recall that one of the seven old tools is the Pareto chart. The classical economist Vilfredo Pareto first observed what has come to be known as the Pareto principle. This principle states that around 80% of all positive results are produced by just 20% of the efforts. Similarly, roughly 80% of all problems can be traced to approximately 20% of all possible causes. It is, then, the critical 20% that one must try to control. Trying to control everything means wasting most of one's time and effort working on the 80% of causes that account for only 20% of the problems.

## Quality Checkpoint 4

The fourth quality checkpoint concerns the quality of incoming materials. The organization must make sure that vendors and suppliers provide materials, products, services, and information of the quality needed. Only then can the organization construct products and deliver services of the quality that its customers desire. QC4, like QC2, is typically emphasized by American organizations. But Deming's criticism of inspection as the primary method used to achieve quality applies to QC4 just as it does to QC2. That is, while inspection at the front door and rear door is necessary, it is often too late. The fifth quality checkpoint is more important.

## Quality Checkpoint 5

Activities at QC5 aim to ensure that input materials, parts, and supplies are designed and produced to specifications. This means working with suppliers and vendors to give them the information they need to deliver materials of the quality that the organization requires. It is not uncommon for an organization committed to TQM to work with its suppliers to design the parts and materials they will deliver to the organization. Many TQM companies send groups of employees to visit suppliers and vendors. These quality action teams help suppliers analyze their own work processes and learn to improve them, using TQM tools. More TQM organizations are, like Motorola, insisting that suppliers adopt a TQM approach.

Deming adamantly emphasizes the importance of QC5. One of his fourteen points exhorts organizations to "end the practice of awarding business on price tag alone." Instead of basing buying decisions on price, Deming advises organizations to find quality-conscious vendors who are responsive to their customers' needs. Organizations should select on the basis of the supplier's record of quality and on its commitment to learn and apply TQM. Then, the supplier can be treated as part of the organization's team.

In Chapter One we commented on Wal-Mart's strategic change from going to the mat with suppliers to negotiate the best deal possible to developing long-term cooperative relationships based on concern for quality. The strategy has paid off by resolving concerns about continuing expansion—as demonstrated when, in 1990, Wal-Mart surpassed Sears as the nation's largest retailer.

Procter & Gamble was one of the suppliers that Wal-Mart first went to, in 1988, to establish a partnership arrangement. P&G found this worked so well that it began a program to develop similar partnerships with other retailer customers, such as Kmart. Both firms have created teams including sales, purchasing, and data processing experts to work together as partners. P&G now has more than 120 such teams working with its customers. In some cases, cash register data goes directly to P&G so that it can track inventory and automatically replenish stock.[14] A wide variety of other large suppliers, including Kraft General Foods, General Mills, Nabisco, and Johnson & Johnson, are active in partnership arrangements. Kraft alone has almost 400 partnership teams.[15]

P&G has found it equally profitable to build partnerships with its own suppliers. The firm has, for example, chosen to develop long-term partnerships with fifteen major trucking firms instead of bidding for the lowest price as was its former practice. P&G estimates that partnerships with suppliers and customers have saved the company about $500 million per year and figures that it can double that savings.[16]

The various activities that occur at QC5 are driven by the needs and desires of customers. This is why the organizations that are most advanced in applying TQM emphasize the connection between QC1 and QC5. They use QC1 information to define the precise characteristics they require of the materials they obtain from their QC5 partners.

## The Quality Management Process

Organizations with a strong focus on quality for the customer recognize and attend to the five quality checkpoints. They also realize that the checkpoints are related in a *circular* rather than in a *linear* fashion. They see QC1 as the most important quality checkpoint, but they also recognize that understanding the connection between QC1 and QC5 is essential.

The cycle shown in Figure 2 is the quality management process.[17] This process is at the heart of how TQM actually operates. Organizations must manage all five quality checkpoints. This means linking customers' needs, wants, and expectations—defined at QC1—to every part of the process, all the way to the suppliers of raw materials. This is a difficult task. It is relatively easy to see how customers' desires define quality as it comes out the door at QC2. It is harder to see how what customers want connects with product design and with control over the manufacturing process (QC3). It is most difficult to carry this all the way to the raw materials at QC4 and to suppliers at QC5.

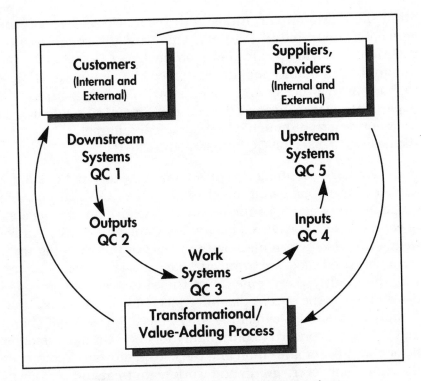

**Figure 2: The Five Quality Checkpoints**

We have tried to illustrate this in Figure 2 by showing arrows going clockwise from supplier to work process to customer. At the same time, the flow of quality checkpoints is counterclockwise, starting with the customer (QC1); continuing to work process output (QC2), the work process itself (QC3), and work process inputs (QC4); and concluding with suppliers (QC5). This makes for difficulty in the quality management process, analogous to the difficulty faced by salmon who must swim upstream against the force of the river's current. And still another level of difficulty is in coordinating and managing the two processes—the actual work flows from suppliers through work systems to customers and the quality management process, which goes in the reverse direction. The two are closely related, yet they flow in opposite directions.

Many Japanese organizations both recognize *and* act on the concepts illustrated in Figure 2. One way is through quality function deployment, an approach designed to translate the importance of quality for the customer (defined at QC1) back to each prior process and checkpoint.[18] Teams, groups, and departments treat those at downstream organizational sites as their customers, although requirements are ultimately based on the desires of external QC1 customers.

For example, a production team's immediate internal customer could be the shipping unit that deals with the team's output. The quality requirements for the production team's output depend, of course, on what external customers want. But those requirements are also determined by the needs of the shipping unit. Its quality needs, too, are based on what external customers want. But the quality requirements of the shipping unit are also determined by the needs of its internal customer, the sales unit. Quality function deployment is, then, based on developing and maintaining a concern about quality for the external customer throughout the organization and the five quality checkpoints. At the same time, every group and work team treats others downstream as internal customers with quality needs that must also be satisfied. In this context, teams become partners working to solve problems and improve quality.

Another way to improve the quality management process is through a technique called *design for manufacture.* This approach fosters new and more effective cross-functional work relationships, especially between engineering and production units. Using the traditional approach, an engineering unit designs a new product and then ships the plans to the production division. But the production unit often encounters problems that engineering design never considered. Solving those problems results in delays and added development costs. Using the design for manufacture technique, the engineering and production units form teams that work together from the start. They jointly develop a design intended to make production as easy as possible.

Bell Labs tried this approach in designing a new circuit board. Normally, design work takes place in New Jersey. Plans are then sent to the assembly plant in Oklahoma, where production begins and problems are resolved as they are encountered. This time, a team was assembled composed of engineers from the New Jersey design unit and the Oklahoma plant. These managers worked together from the start. They worked out every detail in advance. They also anticipated many production problems that would have turned up later and would have cost much more to correct than to avoid. What's more, the overall quality of the product was improved. Compared to an earlier, similar project that had been conducted the old way, the final testing unit found 60% fewer software errors.[19]

Of course, for every unit, upstream or downstream, the most basic and crucial product quality characteristics depend on what the final customer desires—defined, again, at QC1. TQM succeeds only by incorporating a concern about quality for the customer throughout the organization. Some organizations focus on one or another aspect of TQM—for example, quality improvement, key process improvement, satisfaction surveys, or use of various statistical tools. But TQM depends on integrating these and other quality concerns into a coherent and consistent management approach. Only organizations that effectively manage each of he five quality checkpoints as part of a complete, continuous, and constant process will successfully attain TQM. It is an over-riding concern with quality for the customer that drives the process. Tools, techniques, and training are not enough.

## Juran's Approach

Juran describes an approach for designing concern for the customer into organizational operations. His approach creates the sort of quality management process illustrated in Figure 2.[20] Juran's "quality trilogy" of quality planning, quality control, and quality management shows how to plan, coordinate, and integrate a concern for quality into all organizational operations. Juran starts with what he calls a "quality planning road map." We find Juran's directions more useful when presented in words and in some detail rather than visually. The purpose of his map is to build a concern for customers into all organizational operations. The map helps specify just what one does to build such a concern into each of the five quality checkpoints. Juran's road map has six steps, which we have translated into questions and actions.

Step 1: Ask, "Who are our customers? Executives, managers, and employees must first step back and ask who the customer is. They must make a list and then talk to people on the list to see whether they have identified the right people and to ask whether important customers have been left off.

Step 2: Ask customers, "What do you want and need?" Customers' needs and desires are listed and explored in detail. The list is reviewed with other customers to see whether it is correct and complete.

Step 3: Ask, "What do these needs mean to us? The needs and desires that customers described are translated into product and service terms that are meaningful to people within the organization. Again, a list is made. This list is reviewed with employees, modified as needed, translated, and checked for accuracy with customers.

Step 4: Ask, "What are the characteristics of a product/service that satisfies these needs?" Executives, managers, and employees throughout the organization must take the list of customer needs and identify the specific characteristics of products or services that meet them. Again, these product or service descriptions must be checked with customers.

Step 5: Ask, "How do we make this product?" Or ask, "How do we deliver this service?" Actual plans for making products or delivering services are developed in writing and in detail.

Those who must carry out the plans are involved from the start. The plans are shared widely throughout the organization. The focus is always on the question, "How do we do it right the first time?"

*Step 6: Put the plans into operation.* After carrying out the plans, check back with customers to make sure that the products or services have actually satisfied customers' needs.

An emphasis on measurement must be present throughout this six-step process for building customers' needs into organizational operating. What's more, the process is not a one-time-only event. It must be repeated again and again.

An integrated and systemic approach to the quality management process is necessary for TQM to take hold in an organization. Even this, however, is not in itself adequate to sustain TQM over the long run. There is still more to the development and operation of a TQM organization. For the long-term operation of the kind of effective quality management process described in this chapter, an organization must have a *culture* that is based on, that defines, and that supports TQM. This is what Deming calls a *new philosophy of management*. The next chapter examines the nature of this TQM culture, this new philosophy.

## Endnotes

1.  Warren Brown, "GM–Hughes Marriage Awaits a Spark: Defense Firm's Developments May Be Too High-Tech and Too Long-Term for Average Car Buyer," *Washington Post*, April 28, 1991, p. H1.

2.  Joseph M. Juran (Ed.), *Quality Control Handbook* (3rd ed.) (New York: McGraw-Hill, 1974, p. 2-2). Juran, more than others, concentrates on concrete ways to implement this concern for what the customer wants, in terms of a systemic quality management process.

3.  W. Edwards Deming, "Report to Management," *Quality Progress*, July 1972, p. 41.

4.  Armand V. Feigenbaum, quoted in *Boardroom Reports*, April 1, 1991, p. 16. For a more extensive discussion and comparison of various definitions of quality, see David A. Garvin's book *Managing Quality* (New York: Free Press, 1988). In his article "Competing on the Eight Dimensions of Quality" (*Harvard Business Review*, November/December 1987, pp. 101–109), Garvin defines and discusses eight aspects of quality.

5.  Interview with Jeff Maldren of *"CBS Sunday Morning,"* broadcast of April 28, 1991.

6.  The two are not really in direct competition. The Wegmans store closest to Stew Leonard's is more than a hundred miles away.

7.  Michael Barrier, "A New Sense of Service," *Nation's Business*, June 1991, pp. 16–24.

8.  See the work cited in note 7, p. 18.

9.  See the work cited in note 7, p. 19.

10. See the work cited in note 7, p. 19.

11. See the work cited in note 7, p. 19.

12. See the work cited in note 3, p. 2.

13.    A copy of the questionnaire is in Harvey Mackay's book *Swim With the Sharks Without Being Eaten Alive* (New York: William Morrow, 1988).

14.    "Wal-Mart Typifies Cooperation Between Supplier, Retailer." *New York Times News Service,* July 14, 1991.

15.    Barnaby J. Feder, "Procter & Gamble Designs Partnerships to Cut Costs." *New York Times News Service,* July 14, 1991.

16.    See the work cited in note 15.

17.    Our description of the cycle of quality checkpoints derives in part from work by D. Scott Sink and his colleagues at the Virginia Productivity Center. See D. Scott Sink and Thomas C. Tuttle, *Planning and Measurement in Your Organization of the Future* (Norcross, GA: Industrial Engineering and Management Press, 1989).

18.    Joseph M. Juran, *Juran on Planning for Quality* (New York: Free Press, 1988); *Juran on Quality by Design* (New York: Free Press, 1992).

19.    Yoji Akao and Tetsuichi Asaka (Eds.), *Quality Function Deployment: Integrating Customer Requirements into Product Design* (Cambridge, MA: Productivity Press, 1990).

20.    Aaron Bernstein, "Quality Is Becoming Job One in the Office, Too," *Business Week,* April 29, 1991, pp. 54–56.

# 5

# The Cultural Basis of TQM

The hardest part of TQM to understand and apply is the most important part: creating, nurturing, and sustaining a culture based on TQM. But what is *culture*? What are its elements? And how do those elements relate to TQM? These questions go to the heart of the TQM approach. In this chapter we examine the nature of the TQM culture.

## The Nature of Culture

Most social scientists who study organizations agree that culture derives from—perhaps consists of—certain basic beliefs and values. These beliefs and values are defined and expressed through leadership and shared by the members of the organization.

Beliefs involve "if-then" statements. That is, "*If* I do this, *then* that will be the result." For example, a worker knows that statistical quality control data go to the supervisor and then on to the department head. The worker may believe that when it is time for performance appraisals (and rewards) there won't be a raise in the numbers are "bad." The belief is, "If I give them accurate

73

numbers, then they will use those numbers against me." Of course, such a belief (correct or not, and it is more likely than not to be correct) will stifle efforts to apply TQM tools. The worker will only generate and report "good" numbers.

One reason for beliefs that work against TQM can be found in the values they reflect. In the example given, the underlying value is, "People should be controlled by rewarding or punishing them for their performance." This is very different from the value, "Processes should be controlled to result in excellent performance, to produce goods and deliver services of the highest possible quality." The first value has very little to do with organizational performance. The second value relates directly to effective adaptation and achievement of organizational goals and indirectly to the effective coordination of a series of work activities. The most important values and beliefs deal with three crucial areas of organizational functioning: *adapting* to change, *achieving goals*, and *coordinating* the work efforts of employees.

Over the past several years Ford Motor Company has made great strides in quality improvement. Ford has worked with Deming and his associates to begin to build a TQM culture. The company's success is evident in the improved quality of its products. But the original culture, instilled by the founder, did little to help. To give some concrete examples of how organizational values can prevent the effective operation of the three crucial organizational functions, we will look at the culture built by Henry Ford.

Ford was undoubtedly an American business genius. Ford did not, as some think, actually invent the assembly line. Peter Drucker has observed that something like an assembly line was used to construct the great pyramids of ancient Egypt. Still, Ford brought assembly line technology to its highest level of sophistication. And even though one aim was to minimize the level of skill needed by any one worker, Ford paid his employees an unheard of wage for the times, far higher than competitors. He realized that for the company to succeed the average worker had to be able to buy its products, not just make them.

Despite these achievements, Ford had a number of unfortunate idiosyncrasies. Ultimately, his insistence on maintaining control of the company in the face of increasing mental and physical incapacity nearly ruined the firm. And he left Ford Motor Company with a culture based on some very dysfunctional values. Given Ford's unfortunate cultural heritage, the company's achievements of the 1980s and '90s are all the more impressive.

The culture in TQM organizations—that is, the set of shared values and beliefs—makes sure that *adaptive change* aims at fulfilling customers' desires. One reason Ford lost its initial market advantage to General Motors in the 1920s was that Henry Ford refused to develop new models that could compete with those introduced by GM. Ford went on producing his beloved Model T long after competitors had introduced new models of the sort that customers wanted and needed. Ultimately, of course, Ford had to relent and agree to produce the Model A. Legend has it, however, that he stood at the end of the assembly line watching the first Model A roll off. As it passed by, he physically attacked it, beating on the hood with his fists and kicking the door panels. Henry Ford, whose ideas and efforts changed our society, did not like or value some changes.

TQM values define *goal achievement* as meeting customers' needs and desires. Another classic story has Henry Ford responding to a potential customer's query about color availability by saying, "You can have any color you want—as long as it's black." Ford had become so focused on what *he* wanted that he no longer cared about what customers wanted. This view and the cultural value behind it prevailed for another half century and more, as Ford rolled out one of the market disasters of all times: the Edsel. Its design was based only partly on what customers seemed to want at the beginning of the decade. The 1958 Edsel was really intended as a monument to Henry Ford II's late father, Edsel Ford. Founders' values often survive long after they are gone.

The values and beliefs that make up a TQM culture ensure that organization members *cooperate* to carry out their work with a common aim: quality for the customer. But Henry Ford's great invention, the assembly line, is a structural mechanism for *avoiding* cooperative behavior. In contrast, TQM culture is supported by team structures and cross-team partnerships. These devices give people both the need and the opportunity to work together cooperatively in self-managing teams.

If TQM is to develop as an integral element of an organization's culture, a certain set of values and beliefs must be an important part of that culture. Values and beliefs, remember, tell us what is right and what is wrong, as well as the way things happen ("if . . . then . . ."). The values and beliefs that define an organization's culture and direct people's actions must be based on TQM assumptions if they are to support TQM.

Culture is complex. The beliefs and values that make up an organization's culture support and reinforce one another. Often they are interrelated to the point of being interdependent. To understand the bases of TQM culture we can simplify this complex web of TQM culture elements. We have defined each of eight culture elements in terms of a single, specific value or belief. Table 1 shows these eight crucial elements.

The eight sections that follow deal with the TQM culture elements listed in Table 1. At the beginning of each section we restate the specific culture element being examined. We then discuss the meaning of that culture element, often in some detail, giving concrete illustrations of how it looks in action.

| Culture Element 1 | Quality information must be used for improvement, not to judge or control people. |
| Culture Element 2 | Authority must be equal to responsibility. |
| Culture Element 3 | There must be rewards for results. |
| Culture Element 4 | Cooperation, not competition, must be the basis for working together. |
| Culture Element 5 | Employees must have secure jobs. |
| Culture Element 6 | There must be a climate of fairness. |
| Culture Element 7 | Compensation should be equitable. |
| Culture Element 8 | Employees should have an ownership stake. |

**Table 1: Eight Crucial Elements of TQM Culture**

## Culture Element 1: Information for Improvement

Performance and quality information must go to those who use it to understand problems, develop solutions, and take action. Such information must not be used to judge individuals' performance.

Earlier we examined a worker's beliefs about the possible consequences of providing higher-level managers with accurate performance and quality information. These beliefs and their effect illustrated a major obstacle to TQM. That is, most American organizations use performance and quality information not to improve performance and quality but in an attempt to control employees. They monitor and evaluate employees to make sure they "do it right" or, at least that they do what management wants them to. With this aim in mind, management uses rewards for good results and punishments for bad results.

This practice goes directly against Deming's key principle, *"Drive out fear."* Organizations that try to control employees' performance by reward and punishment make it certain that employees will not share accurate performance and quality information with management. After all, who would want to give higher-level management information that resulted in negative outcomes for the person providing the data?

Too often, quality information goes up the hierarchy to a person's boss or even higher and the data are tied to that person as a "cause." This signals that the purpose of the performance and quality measurement system is to control individual employees through rewards and sanctions. Such systems aim to control people, not to improve performance and quality. TQM has very little chance of succeeding under these conditions.

One term for this type of measurement is *"results metric."* That is, the metric or measure assesses final results or outcomes. The idea is similar to the old inspection approach to quality control. That approach, we now know, is limited by the kinds of corrections and improvements to work processes that can be made. Moreover, it cannot lead to *continuous improvement* in processes, to result in high quality products and services. But even final inspection at QC2 has some use in TQM. Using results metrics to judge employees' performance has no benefit of any kind for TQM.

It is now possible for supervisors to monitor employees' activities to a degree unknown and unimagined just a few years ago. Scholars have even debated as to whether management could or should "recentralize" decision making and control by making use of such data collection approaches. For example, most of us are familiar with the approach used in many telephone companies to monitor the length of time operators spend with customers. The purpose is to reduce the length of each call, thus increasing efficiency. In this case results metrics go directly to the supervisor. Supervisors tell operators to reduce the amount of time spent on each call. But the measure tells nothing about the causes of calls that last longer than the maximum permissible time.

Bell Canada was one of the companies that instituted monitoring for what was thought to be quality control. It didn't work well. Employees—and the union—complained. In response the company designed an experiment involving 2400 operators in Ontario. Operators were monitored as a group. Individual times were no longer recorded, only the group's distribution and average. In the past when an operator's average time went above the desired standard of 23 seconds the employee would be disciplined. In the experiment, when the group average went up, managers met with employees to review the data, explore the problem, and develop a solution. Productivity went up and stayed up. The vast majority of employees thought that they were delivering better service, and the numbers backed them up. The experiment was extended throughout Bell Canada.[1]

In most Japanese organizations process performance data go only as far as the person whose job it is to use that information to maintain and improve performance and quality. Data reported up the line on quality problems and actions taken to resolve them may be aggregated and examined by higher levels of management, but such information cannot normally be traced to one or another worker or team. *"Process metrics"* is a term used to describe this approach to the use of performance and quality data by those who can apply it directly to identify problems, solve them, and make improvements. That is, the measurements center on the process of work, not just on the outcomes.

At times management does need quality control information concerning what Deming calls common causes of quality problems. Common causes are part of the production process that management designed and set up. They are not the result of undesired variation introduced by the worker or by some other factors, which Deming refers to as special causes. Workers must have the authority, as well as the responsibility, to use measurement tools to identify and eliminate special causes. But management must go farther and "empower" workers with the authority to identify and act on their own initiative to correct common causes of variation—the source of most quality problems.

Measurement systems designed to support TQM must be focused on improvement of processes, not on control of those responsible for work processes. This means emphasizing process metrics, not results metrics. The aim is to assess and improve work processes by identifying and correcting factors that cause undesired variation. This is very different from the notion of controlling *people.* The way in which measurement systems are designed and used determines whether employees support or subvert a TQM effort. Measurement system design and use is a crucial determinant of whether an organization's approach will succeed or fail.

Like managers at Bell Canada, Federal Express managers were concerned about the time telephone customer service agents were spending on each call. And, like Bell Canada, FedEx began a program of monitoring. Half of an agent's performance appraisal rating was based on doing better than the standard time of 140 seconds per call. But employees and their managers began to complain. Performance wasn't getting better, it was getting worse. Agents had to be curt and abrupt with customers to "make the numbers." Top management listened and abandoned the fruitless employee-control-oriented results metrics program. Instead, a supervisor listens at random to each agent just twice a year. Soon afterward, the two meet to discuss what the supervisor heard. The emphasis is on customer service quality. Time is not mentioned. Service has improved since the new approach was put into use while the average call has decreased in length.[2]

In systems that use process metrics to emphasize measurement for product or service improvement, the persons responsible for doing the job are the ones who collect and use the quality information. No one else needs such information, at least not in a form that can be traced to an individual. This is because workers themselves use the performance and quality information that they have collected to solve the problems that they have identified.

Organizations with measurement systems that focus on monitoring people's performance, relying on results metrics, present a dramatic contrast. A state of management by fear often exists: If your numbers aren't good enough, you'll be punished. In such systems the point of gathering performance and quality data is not to identify problems and solve them. Instead, management's concern is controlling workers, usually by punishing those thought responsible for quality problems.

Designing and using measurement systems to control employees instead of to understand and improve processes is stupid as well as self-defeating. As noted earlier, most quality problems can be attributed to the way in which work processes are set up (common causes), not to errors made by workers (special causes). Deming estimates that about 94% of all problems (that is, sources of uncontrolled variation) are due to common causes attributable to the system and not to workers. He believes that only about 6% of all problems are due to special causes that might be traced to employees.

Others put the ratio of common to special causes at 90/10, 85/15, 80/20, or some other set of numbers. These are all guesses. The true proportions are not really important. The crucial point is that a large—probably a very large—proportion of all quality problems is due to the system, not to the actions of employees. The work processes were created by management and they are management's responsibility. You cannot improve quality by controlling people. This is even more the case when employees are not permitted or able to change or correct the work processes and systems that they must use. Trying to control people also reinforces the wrong value: getting the right numbers, no matter what. That does nothing to improve performance and quality.

Not only does the attempt to control people reinforce the wrong values and beliefs, it also results in a deadly by-product: fear. Deming refers to fear as the great enemy of quality improvement in any organization.[3] If one is afraid that poor performance or bad numbers will result in sanctions—low pay raise, no pay raise, a reprimand, a reduction in pay, or even loss of one's job—then no one is likely to provide management with bad numbers. In such situations, workers quickly learn that the only important job is producing good numbers. Making high quality products or delivering high quality services becomes irrelevant. In this way high quality, excellent performance, and customer satisfaction—the essential elements of goal achievement—become almost irrelevant. Only *looking* good is important.

## Culture Element 2: Authority Equal to Responsibility

Employees responsible for doing the work and attaining certain outcomes must have the authority they need to carry out their responsibilities effectively.

Those responsible for hands-on production or service activities must also have authority to take positive actions based on performance and quality information. This means making process control—production and service assessment and improvement—a basic part of employees' jobs. People must have the authority to control and improve the work for which they are responsible.

This culture element is based on the value that employees should control their own work activities rather than following orders from above or performing a set of mindless, rote actions. In the language of modern human resource management, the term most often heard is "empowerment." That is, employees should have the authority to take actions that will lead to high quality and excellent performance. They should not have to obtain approval from above for every minor change that might be made in some set of standard procedures.

American organizations, both large and small, have discovered that empowering employees can have striking, positive effects. A worker at an IBM plant in Rochester, Minnesota, spotted a defect on a computer storage device and shut down the line. This saved IBM the cost of correcting defects as well as the potentially greater cost of lost customer satisfaction. This IBM facility won the 1990 Malcolm Baldrige National Quality Award from the U.S. Department of Commerce.[4]

At a smaller operation, Johnsonville Foods in Sheboygan, Wisconsin, teams of empowered workers buy equipment, write budgets, train one another, cut their hours when necessary, and even hire and fire one another.[5] This sort of team operation, often called "self-managing" or "autonomous" teams, is becoming more common.[6] Johnsonville Foods' owner Ralph Strayer says "It isn't a soft or crazy deal. I'm a real hard-nosed pragmatic guy. . . . Teach people to do for themselves; this way you get a far better performance." The figures back him up: Since he empowered employees, sales have increased by more than 20% per year and productivity has increased 50% in the past four years. Rejects went from 5% to less than one-half of 1%.

Federal Express won another 1990 Baldrige Award, the first service company to compete successfully for the award. Tom Peters tells a now legendary story about a "junior telecommunications expert":

who, following a blizzard in the California Sierras, was faced
with the prospect of having no phone service for several days.
. . . With . . . no need to seek approval from above he rented a
helicopter (using his personal American Express card), was
dropped onto a snowbound mountaintop, trudged three-
quarters of a mile in chest-deep snow, and fixed the line to get
FedEx back in business.[7]

Peters goes on to note that while this behavior was extraordinary,
it was no fluke accident in that "all workers are routinely expected
to take whatever initiative is required to fix problems and/or
extend first-rate service to a customer."[8] That sort of expectation
has always been characteristic of Federal Express. But what
of organizations in which such expectations have never before
existed?

Even a company that has not traditionally given employees
authority can change. Up until 1980, Johnsonville Foods was
run like most other companies: Ralph Strayer, the owner and
CEO, made all the decisions. Despite continued growth and
profitability he was worried; employees didn't seem to care about
their work. Mistakes and accidents were on the increase. Incorrect
ingredients were added to a product; a forklift was driven through
a wall.

Strayer wanted a company in which everyone took responsibility
—for the job, the product, and the company. But an attitude
survey demonstrated that the opposite was the case, just as he
had observed. After much thought, Strayer concluded that
employees were justified. He had made all the decisions; everyone else was just a hired hand. It took him two years to begin to
change, by giving people the authority they needed to carry out
their responsibilities effectively.

In one plant, Strayer reports,[9] employees were unhappy about
having to work weekends to meet deadlines. He asked plant
managers to get the workers to figure out why weekend work was

needed. They found that machine downtime averaged between 30% and 40% during the week. The most important causes were absenteeism, people arriving late for their work shifts, and other factors that employees could control. By addressing these causes, employees reduced downtime to 10%; weekend work became unnecessary.

It took Ralph Strayer several more years more to involve employees fully in making work decisions, to empower them to deal with common as well as with special causes. In concrete terms, employees gained authority over their own work, from tasting the sausage for quality to analyzing and solving production problems. Over the course of a decade, Strayer moved the organization's culture from one of authoritarian control to one of employee involvement based on total quality management. Of course, the sort of authority changes described here are just part of the more comprehensive changes that Strayer instigated, including changes in the pay system, the appraisal system, and the hierarchy itself.

The manager of an employee-run cereal plant points out, "Nobody knows the job as well as those doing it. If you empower those people to make the decisions they make good ones." She goes on to say, "It's not a social experiment. It makes good business sense." When employees are empowered to make decisions they often save the company substantial sums of money. At Chaparral Steel, in Texas, a lathe worker found a new machine that cost only half the $1.5 million that had been budgeted. Substantial quality improvements can occur when employees have the authority— are empowered—not just to identify problems but to make decisions and take actions on their own initiative to solve problems.

These are examples in which experienced and capable employees were able to use their knowledge to make good decisions. Simply giving people authority to make decisions and take actions does not mean that their decisions will be good ones or that their actions will be effective. For empowerment to have positive effects, employees must also be *enabled*. That is, they must have the knowledge and skill needed to use their authority well.

Enabling employees means providing them with training in TQM concepts and applications as well as in the use of statistical tools for quality control and improvement. There are other, less obvious, training needs if employees are to be effectively enabled as well as empowered. For example, new teams created to apply TQM methods, either on an ad hoc task force basis or as permanent work groups, often need to learn how to work effectively as a group. Employees who are enabled *and* empowered have the knowledge, skills, and opportunity to take corrective actions to solve problems and make improvements.

There is still another limit on empowering employees and teams. When work process problems involve other employees or teams, those others must also have a say. This point is important because many problems arise at organizational interfaces— the points at which one work process must be coordinated with another. Recall that the TQM management process described in Chapter Four calls for each employee or team to consider the next person or group downstream as the customer for that person's or group's output. Ensuring quality for the customer means making sure that the customer's needs and desires are known and that this knowledge is the basis for action. This principle applies to internal customers as well as to final, external customers.

Empowering employees and creating self-managing teams can be a frightening prospect for some managers. Many fear that they will lose their jobs when teams no longer have formal supervisors. While this has happened in some cases, the reason is not usually elimination of the job. More often, managers lose their jobs when self-managing teams are developed because they cannot perform the new roles of facilitator and coach. Other managers are concerned (sometimes unconsciously) more with losing control than with losing their jobs. What they fail to realize is that control based on formal authority is really very weak. Effective leaders know that one gains far more control by empowering others and, in a sense, giving away one's formal authority. When self-managing teams are used effectively they actually increase the total amount of control and influence in an organization and lead to increased effectiveness.[10]

## Culture Element 3: Rewards for Results

There must be rewards for results. Individuals, teams, and all members of the organization must share equitably the fruits of their efforts.

TQM requires that achievement be recognized, both symbolically and in terms of material rewards. All too often rewards are merely symbolic—a certificate, a pin, or the employee's name on a plaque or in a newsletter story. This sort of symbolic recognition is important, and we aren't suggesting that it be eliminated. However, symbolic rewards should be accompanied by material rewards such as cash bonuses or special privileges that employees see as important. It is also important for concrete rewards to be joined with symbolic rewards. Such linkage reinforces the values being rewarded in an open and obvious manner, making those values stronger and more widespread among the organization's members.

Material rewards support and reinforce the value that it is good to achieve high quality and productivity or that problem solving (effective adaptation) is good. If such achievements are good, one would wonder why management fails to reward them. If problem solving is important, one must ask why management's recognition of effective examples is limited to symbolic rewards.

Eventually, one realizes that such achievements in quality, productivity, or problem solving are *not* in fact valued.

Even when material rewards are used, they are often not used well. Rewards should exist at multiple levels, that is, at the organizational level, at the group level, and at the individual level. In the United States rewards are often directed only to the individual. And when teams as well as individuals are rewarded, the system is often set up so that a conflict is created. Moreover, rewards are often attached to the wrong values, values that do not support effective, adaptive problem solving, achievements in quality and productivity, or smoothly coordinated teamwork.

In Japan, a firm's good performance (as measured by productivity and profit) frequently yields a bonus to employees equivalent to a substantial portion of their yearly salary.[11] Thus, recognition for achievement occurs on the organizational level. In the United States, too, more organizations are trying out formal plans for sharing the results of improvement efforts with employees and thus rewarding employees for results. One especially well-known type of system is the Scanlon Plan, but there are many other formal gainsharing approaches.[12]

Gainsharing involves sharing with all employees some portion of the measurable gains in performance, productivity, and profit that are achieved as a result of employees' efforts to find ways to do jobs as well or better while reducing costs. The reductions may be achieved by increasing efficiency, reducing waste, or inventing new and better ways to get the job done. All gainsharing plans rely on some concrete, data-based approach to identify (or estimate) the actual gain to the organization from such efforts on the part of employees. This gain is then shared with employees, often as a bonus calculated on the basis of an agreed-on formula.

Profit sharing is different from gainsharing. Employees are simply given some share of the organization's profit, as a bonus, often on an annual, semiannual, or quarterly basis. A profit-sharing system may simply state that 10% of pretax profits are to be distributed among all employees in proportion to their regular wages. There is no attempt to link the amount of profit shared to the savings or profit gain attributable to employees' improvement efforts.

Globe Metallurgical, in Alabama, applied Deming's approach to win the 1988 Baldrige Award. Globe also reported quality-related savings of $10.3 million per year. This savings permitted raises averaging 6% per year and profit-sharing payments of about $4000 per year for each employee. Johnsonville Foods also has a profit sharing system as well as extensive employee involvement. Tom Peters reports that market share in the Milwaukee area rose from 7% to 50% over a recent ten-year period.[13]

When Virginia Fibre Corporation (VFC), a paper manufacturer, began operations in 1975, its founder Bob Macauley knew that he wanted to create a different kind of organization. He wanted everyone to be treated with dignity and respect and to feel free to help one another, with no restrictions on the tasks that one or another employee might be permitted to do. He and VFC president Charlie Chandler realized that to attain the level of employee involvement and commitment they wanted, the organization would have to allow everyone to share in its growth and performance. They created an organization based on what they call the "Principles of the partnership." Included was a system for sharing with employees the financial gain that resulted from their performance and productivity improvements.

Management estimated how many tons of paper the machinery could produce per day and set that as the base. Each month the average daily tonnage produced is calculated. For every ten tons over the base, everyone in the company receives a 1% bonus. The bonus is paid to every person from the chairman to the most recently hired permanent employee.[14] This past year the firm had two successive months in which the bonus was more than 20% of monthly wages.

In some cases reward and profit-sharing plans work at the group rather than at the organizational level. This is true, for example, of the TQM program at Motorola. Rewards go to teams or groups of employees for their team efforts and achievements rather than to everyone in the organization.

All this contrasts with the standard approach to rewarding employees in the United States, which operates on an individual basis. Organizations practicing TQM use this approach, too. However, they apply it in ways that are very different from the merit pay and performance appraisal approach common in American industry. For example, Johnsonville Foods, which ties bonuses to company performance (sharing almost 30% of pretax profits), also provides for individual rewards. While the firm gives no automatic cost-of-living or seniority raises, employees can increase their salaries by assuming greater responsibility. In some other organizations, pay is based partly on employees' skills. That is, in order to receive a pay increase an employee documents and demonstrates that his or her value to the firm has increased as a result of learning certain new skills.

Some would argue that a true TQM system need not include a purely individual reward element. We disagree. Even in Japan, recognition rewards occur both on the individual and group level. For example, workers in some firms receive a small payment for *any* improvement suggestion, with larger payments for exceptionally good ideas.[15] This supports the value of solving problems and coming up with ideas that result in effective adaptation.

Suggestion systems are among the most common mechanisms used to reward employees. The average American firm with some sort of suggestion system receives about one suggestion for every seven employees, per year. In contrast, in Japan Mitsubishi gets about *100* ideas per employee per year, Canon gets *70*, and Pioneer Electronics gets *60*. It is not, then, uncommon for a Japanese firm to get *six to ten thousand times* as many suggestions per employee per year as do American organizations.

Of course, Japanese organizations use group rewards as well as individual and organizational rewards. They often do so by rewarding quality circles (QCs) composed of work teams for their contributions to quality improvement. Unlike the American experience discussed in Chapter One, QCs have been generally effective and valuable in Japan. Quality circles are, at heart, simply small-group suggestion systems.

But Japanese firms don't set up QCs simply by telling groups of workers to meet once a week. Musashi Semiconductor (a division of Hitachi Corporation) spent years creating a culture and building the small-group skills needed to develop good suggestions. The system went far beyond the sort of QC set-up commonly installed in U.S. firms. Only after six years was the first group-developed improvement proposal received. In the next year over 26,000 were received, almost 100,000 in the following year, and more than double that during the third year. Of the 112,000 improvement proposals submitted during the last six months of the third year, almost 100,000—87.8%, to be exact—were implemented.

This was possible because, having built the cultural base for employee involvement and collaboration, the organization did not have to spend a great deal of time carefully examining the proposals to make sure that each one was acceptable to management and consistent with organizational policies. The groups had already done that. Only proposals requiring major capital expenditures or involving other work units needed management approval. Musashi *empowered* employees, but first the company *enabled* them. It helped employees develop new skills while establishing a culture that guided them in the wise use of their authority. Despite what appear to be the impressive results of this program, the Musashi groups achieved only the *average* when their result were compared with those of all the other groups in Hitachi![16]

Individual rewards work best when they avoid pitting employees one against the other for a fixed quantity of money. Still, rewarding individuals for improvement suggestions while at the same time using quality circles to generate improvement ideas—and receiving team rewards for doing so—works well in Japanese firms. This is so even though individuals' motivation to attain personal rewards through individual suggestions may conflict with a team motivation to come up with suggestions that result in rewards for all team members. In American organizations, however, such inconsistency in reward systems would surely create problems (assuming, that is, that the American organization had both an individually rewarded suggestion system and a quality circle plan based on team rewards for effective improvement ideas).

More than a decade ago, Geert Hofstede, a Dutch organizational researcher, studied IBM divisions in forty countries around the world.[17] Through surveys he collected a massive amount of data from more than 100,000 individuals. Using these data Hofstede identified a set of culture dimensions along which organizations could be compared. On one dimension, individualism, the American part of IBM scored higher than any other unit in any other country. Thus, in the United States, where the value of individualism is greater than almost anywhere else in the world, it is unrealistic to think that organizations can ignore individual motivation.

Hofstede's work highlights the need for careful and detailed planning in developing and implementing reward systems (and continuously improving them). It is much more difficult to develop multilevel reward systems operating at the individual, group, and organization levels than it is to construct systems that function at just one level, be it individual, team, or organization. Japanese organizational culture lessens this difficulty, while American organizational culture makes it even greater. In American organizations reward systems must be designed with special care to avoid forcing individuals into competitive conflicts with their own team efforts.

American Airlines does this by sharing any awards among all employees who participate in putting a suggestion into practice, which means the person who made the suggestion as well as that person's supervisor. Employees consider this "IdeAAs in Action" award program a valuable benefit, second only to profit sharing. The program director reports receiving about 300 suggestions a day.[18]

We have emphasized the importance of designing reward systems that use all three forms of reward—individual, team, and organizational. Still, we must point out the special importance of team-based rewards. They are important because they strengthen and support work teams. Work teams in turn represent the single most effective way to structure an organization for TQM. We don't mean temporary teams set up to analyze and correct problems and composed of people who do not work with one another on a constant, day-to-day basis. We refer to organizing or reorganizing work so that tasks are the responsibility of permanent self-managing teams, teams that have the authority needed to do the job. Such teams provide a structural basis for cooperation, which then becomes not just an ideal but a necessity.

Most American organizations take the easy way out when designing reward systems: They use mostly or solely individual rewards. This makes most American firms susceptible to Deming's deadly disease of individual merit rating and annual performance appraisal. This type of reward system has several negative effects. First, it emphasizes individual competition. Thus, when one person receives a very positive rating, it often means that others must receive a low rating to maintain a normal distribution.

But the notion of a normal distribution of work performance is not only false, it helps guarantee that overall performance will be less than is possible. That is, the assumption that performance must conform to a normal distribution, a "bell-shaped curve," places an artificial limit on performance. It directs attention toward comparisons between "good" and "poor" individual performers, that is, persons above or below the average. But this is not the relevant issue. TQM is a key to unlocking productivity and quality gains by raising the absolute level of system performance, by raising the average itself.

To do this, Virginia Fibre focuses on team as well as individual objectives and accomplishments. But this is very rare. One study of the performance appraisal practices of twenty organizations known nationally for their TQM efforts found that all but one had performance appraisal systems. And while about half had made some modifications to the traditional individual merit rating approach, not one had developed a team approach for rewarding performance, not even the organizations that were making extensive use of team operations.[19]

Individual performance ratings naturally lead to comparisons between and among employees. This in turn reinforces competition. In such cases, says Deming, "Instead of working for the company, people compete with each other."[20] When organizations rely on individual appraisal and merit ratings to assign rewards, employees will often forgo opportunities for productive collaboration and cooperation. Instead, they engage in actions that will make them look better as individuals. The individual result is a higher performance rating—and a greater pay increase or bonus. But for the organization the outcome may be low-quality products and lower profits.

The individual merit rating approach to reward, as traditionally applied, encourages the use of quality information to judge individuals. In this way information that might be used productively, for quality control and improvement, is made worthless. Information used to evaluate an individual—for example, to demonstrate one's achievements in an appraisal interview—is certain to be distorted in the positive direction. How else would one have the appearance of effective performance? When such use of information is encouraged, the use of information for quality improvement is discouraged. No one wants to risk sharing information that might prove he or she has problems.

Deming and some of his followers[21] argue that organizations must simply do away with performance appraisal. But this is not realistic, necessary, or even desirable. We have, like Deming, argued against merit rating and performance appraisal as traditionally used. Especially damaging is the use of quality information to judge individuals. It may seem that we are contradicting the culture element being described, based as it is on the value of rewards for results. At the least, one might conclude that there should only be rewards for group or team performance and for all employees based on organizational performance. This is not so.

American culture *requires* that individuals be rewarded for their achievements. And individual performance *can* be rewarded in a manner consistent with and supportive of TQM. We've already suggested several ways that this can be done. Moreover, people both need and want feedback about their performance that lets them know how they are doing in ways that can help them improve.

In order to provide accurate information that is useful for improvement, such performance feedback must be nonjudgmental and it must be unrelated to the reward system. It is a mistake to confuse performance *appraisal* with performance *feedback*. We concur with those who would do away with appraisal. At the same time, we recognize the importance of providing people with descriptive performance feedback, information they can use to understand and analyze performance problems as well as to make improvements in the quality of their own performance.

When the reward system, especially at the individual level, is separate from the performance feedback system, then individual rewards for individual performance will not conflict with the use of information for quality improvement. Individual rewards can be based on skill improvement, on the development of new skills, on quality improvement ideas and actions, or on a variety of other performance-relevant factors. The only limit is the imagination of managers and employees. Individual rewards should not, however, be based on the assessment of individual productivity or on measures of quality of the product or service that are tied to the individual. Rewards must be designed to recognize the contributions of individuals to organizational performance, not as tools to control their behavior.

In sum, there are two important aspects to this culture element. *First*, employees must share in the outcomes of their efforts. This means that there should be both material as well as symbolic rewards for the results that employees have helped to achieve. *Second*, rewards should be designed at all levels, that is, for individuals, for groups or teams, and for everyone (based on organizational performance and outcomes). It is difficult to design a multilevel reward system in which there is no conflict among individual, team, and organization-level rewards, but it is far from impossible. Rewards, both symbolic and material, are limited only by people's imagination and creativity. The key is consistency among individual, group, and organizational rewards. Achieving such consistency is often a challenge.

## Culture Element 4: Cooperation, Not Competition

Cooperation must be the basis for working together. To the extent possible, people in an organization must support one another's efforts, not compete with one another.

As we have just discussed, all too often U.S. organizations reward employees for individual efforts but not for actions that contribute to team or organizational performance. Even worse, rewards often accrue to a person when that individual's actions are detrimental to the performance of the group or the organization. Earlier we quoted Deming, who pointed out that in Japanese organizations everyone acts as part of a team, for the good of the entire organization. In American organizations it is often a matter of every person for him- or herself.

One way to move away from competition and toward greater cooperation is to design jobs so that employees work in teams. Such change is happening all over the United States and in almost every industry. This started in the late 1960s as experiments in new plant design using "sociotechnical systems." The work was set up to be done by teams, operating with a high degree of authority and autonomy—and with no formal supervisors. In the early days some of these experiments floundered but by the late 1970s there were hundreds of successes. By the late 1980s they numbered in the thousands.

Richard Walton, of the Harvard Business School, has been active in these experiments from the very start. He reports that over the past twenty years there has been a clear movement in American organizations away from efforts to control workers and toward reliance on employees' commitment.[22] Walton sees this as closely connected to the increasing use of self-controlling work teams. Joseph Juran suggests that a major trend for the 1990s will be an even greater emphasis on these self-managing teams.[23]

A recent survey of Fortune 1000 firms substantiates Juran's prediction. The survey showed that 46% of those responding had some self-managing teams. In 1987 the figure was only 27%.[24] Johnsonville Foods uses the self-managing team approach along with employee empowerment. One team even designed its assembly line. Juran has observed that when workers design or redesign their own jobs this restores planning to where it once was—and still belongs—at the operational level. And, Juran points out, planning by work teams is much more sophisticated than planning entirely by management.[25] Management on its own cannot build a concern for quality into every organizational operation at all five quality checkpoints. Only when employees are actively involved, enabled, and empowered can this aim be met.

Team-based job design supports the value of authority equal to the group's responsibilities. Another effect is to make it more difficult (as well as unnecessary) for managers to try to use results metrics to reward or coerce individual employees to achieve better performance outcomes. At the same time, team-based job design helps to create and maintain a reward system that is tied to accomplishments—team accomplishments.

In Japan the cooperative team ethic is so strong that workers see themselves as team members even when tasks have not been designed to be performed by a group of people working together. In the United States the value of individualism is so strong that it will take quite a lot of effort to develop the value of cooperation that seems to come so easily in Japan.

While efforts to strengthen the value of cooperation are important, this does not mean that it is necessary to eliminate competition completely. In any case, that would be impossible. It's foolish to attempt such a radical change in the basic cultural assumptions that are common to American society and reflected in American organizations. Two specific important examples are (1) the belief that individuals should be rewarded (equitably) for their achievements and (2) the value of competition.

Culture elements can be moderated and balanced, for example, by developing reward systems that focus on the team and the entire organization as well as on the individual. Jobs can be redesigned in ways that make them collaborative team activities rather than work performed by isolated individuals. It is, however, pointless to try to reverse existing values and beliefs, for example, by linking all rewards to team and organizational performance or by eliminating competition. Still, some have made impassioned arguments for such radical changes.[26]

Some followers of Deming argue that competition is counterproductive whether inside an organization or outside. Rafael Aguayo, for example, seems to oppose all competition, including competition for customers and market.[27] Such an argument is not viable, simply because the basic economic system in the United States will not change from a competitive market basis to a system based purely on cooperation.

We do not mean to discourage cooperation at any level. Deming tells organizations to cooperate by teaching others, even competitors, about TQM. To an extent, this idea has taken hold. Many TQM organizations, for example, look to others inside and outside of their own industries to identify best practices, referred to as "benchmarks." While some organizations still refuse to share information about "how it's done," many more are coming to recognize that such sharing is good for everyone and that such information need not be considered proprietary, to be kept secret in order to maintain the firm's competitive advantage.

It is neither realistic nor reasonable to expect American organizations or American society in general to abandon competition. It is, however, both realistic and true that organizations are coming to recognize the advantages of collaboration and cooperation, internally and externally. One interesting signal is a recent, widely publicized agreement between IBM and Apple.[28] Instead of continuing the decade-old competition based on incompatible computers, the two firms have agreed to develop new technology jointly that will permit future products to use common operating software.

New ideas and approaches can be adapted and integrated within familiar cultural patterns. This is in part what Peter Drucker meant when he said, in a recent *Wall Street Journal* essay, "Don't change corporate culture—use it!"[29] This is exactly what Japan has done with Western innovations. And the Japanese started not in the 1940s with Deming but in the 1870s with rapid industrialization under the Meiji emperor. Their efforts extend right up to the present time, with the acceptance of Western political, governmental, and business forms that actually contain within them (sometimes openly and sometimes covertly) very traditional cultural elements.[30] Instead of trying to alter strong cultural values and beliefs in radical ways, American organizations might do better to emulate the Japanese and adapt and integrate new ideas and practices within existing cultural patterns.

---

## Culture Element 5: Job Security

Employees must know that their jobs are secure, that they will not be discarded at management's convenience like an obsolete piece of equipment.

Japanese firms are known for their reluctance to lay off employees, even under the most adverse business conditions. A surprising number of the very best American firms, such companies as Hewlett-Packard (HP) and Eli Lilly, have long adopted the same practice of no layoffs. HP has not laid off an employee since it was founded more than fifty years ago. Founder Bill Hewlett explains, "We didn't want a 'hire and fire' company."[31] Eli Lilly's record of no layoffs extends back more than a hundred years. Such policies are probably the most powerful strategy for organizations wishing to drive out fear.[32]

An individual with years of experience as corporate director of training for a very large retailing conglomerate told us that security goes beyond guarantees against layoffs. In many organizations, this person noted, the common adage is, "Screw up the first time and I'll get you. Screw up the second time and you're history!" Instead, what is needed is the commitment of managers at all levels to do everything possible and reasonable to coach employees to success. Too many American businesses treat employees like inventory that can be replaced at will. But only when employees feel a sense of job security will they take risks to make improvements. At a time when many organizations are downsizing by eliminating jobs, employees' fear of making mistakes that might cost them their jobs can greatly reduce their potential effectiveness.

Many organizations are hesitant to make commitments that top managers feel might be impossible to meet. What if, despite the best of intentions, the firm finds no economic alternative to reducing the size of its work force? One way to deal with this is to make job security an implicit rather than an explicit commitment. Organizations can emphasize that job security depends not on individual assessment but on *organizational* performance. Rubbermaid makes this an open commitment, stating that the reward for productivity is job security. This strategy contrasts with the typical adversarial relationship between management and workers that leads employees to believe that increases in productivity will lead to layoffs. Ample evidence, however, suggests that the opposite is actually true: Increased productivity means more, not fewer, jobs.[33]

This inference appears to be logically as well as economically sound. That is, performance determines organizational security and survival. How can jobs be more secure than the organization? However, the organization must share financial information with employees. Only then can everyone see and understand the economic reality. Employees can then examine the economic evidence that might justify personnel cuts. And if reductions really are necessary, employees can share in making decisions about which jobs to eliminate and how to do so.

U.S. management has often viewed performance and productivity improvement as a matter of driving down costs. This, too, has negative effects on job security. Labor force reductions, which require the same or more work to be done by fewer employees, are an obvious way to reduce costs. The belief that it will at times be necessary to eliminate jobs to reduce costs may be why so few American firms provide secure jobs. But these assumptions about reducing costs are false. Research and practice show that the best way to improve performance *and* reduce costs is to focus on quality improvement, with an emphasis on what customers desire. Peter Drucker has observed that work must be done right or not done. Trying to get something done cheaply by using inferior materials and hoping that it will be all right is foolish.[34]

Quality and cost are often thought of as in conflict: The greater the emphasis on quality, the more costs increase. This, however, is a false assumption. In *The Reckoning,* David Halberstam tells of a Ford executive who observed that Japanese auto plants had no areas reserved for reworking defects; they did not need them. That observation led the executive to rethink the problem and calculate how much could be saved by not having to correct defects, by getting it right the first time. He was surprised to find that the cost of correcting defects was between 20% and 40% of Ford's revenues. The savings obtained by doing the work right the first time would, he concluded, be far more than any possible increase in manufacturing costs. As the title of a recent popular book asks, "If you don't have the time to do it right the first time, when will you find the time to do it over?[35]

Asserting that increasing quality increases costs is "an argument from ignorance," according to Deming. That's because only costs that can be accounted for are considered. Other, unknown costs *decrease* with an increase in quality, for example, the cost of losing a customer due to poor quality. Such cost decreases may be far more important and substantial than any increases. One consulting firm[36] reports that more than 80% of customer losses are due to poor quality of the product or service. And, this firm points out, it costs five times as much to get a new customer as it does to retain an existing one. In their article "Zero Defections,"

Frederick R. Reichheld and W. Earl Sasser, Jr.,[37] report that for the various service organizations they studied, which included banks, auto repair shops, insurance companies, laundries, and shipping and distribution firms, a 5% decrease in customer "defections" would represent an increase in profit of 25% to 85%.

It is shortsighted to seek to cut costs by cutting corners. It is even more self-defeating to try to reduce costs by laying off employees. Doing so shows that the organization does not value people. In Chapter One we gave the example of a firm in which a quality circle program failed after half the work force was laid off. Some organizations start such programs as a cost reduction technique, not because of a commitment to quality. It is difficult to imagine why employees who see their coworkers laid off to reduce costs would want to help the organization make a better product or deliver a better service.

Paradoxically, trying to reduce costs by eliminating people can have just the opposite effect. People who feel that their jobs are at risk are not likely to spend their time looking for ways to reduce costs. In fact, they may create new (and unnecessary) activities to make themselves look less dispensable, thus adding new costs. Organizations that do not provide employees with secure jobs are unlikely to find success through TQM.

---

## Culture Element 6: A Climate of Fairness

Everyone in the organization must perceive that a climate of fairness exists, based on the behaviors and actions of managers at all levels.

Recent research shows that by their actions managers create organizational "climates." These climates can be characterized as fair or unfair, as seen by employees. But fairness is a much more complex issue than many people assume. Some of the most respected philosophers, from ancient times (for example, Aristotle in the *Nicomachean Ethics*) to the present (for example, John Rawls in *A Theory of Justice*), have struggled to define the nature of fairness. Part of the problem is that fairness is in the eye of the beholder. Two people can look at the same situation and one can judge it as grossly unfair while the other finds nothing amiss. The solution is simple in one way and complicated in another.

The simple part is that fairness depends mostly on managers' actual behaviors, especially the behaviors of top-level leaders. Managers can choose to act in ways that create a positive climate of fairness. The complex part is that acting is far more difficult than deciding, because it involves interrelated behaviors that require skill and practice. Ten specific areas of action help to define the organizational climate of fairness:

- actions that develop *trust*, such as sharing useful information and making good on commitments

- acting *consistently*, so that employees are not surprised or taken aback by unexpected management actions or decisions

- being scrupulously *truthful* and avoiding so-called white lies and actions designed to manipulate others by giving a certain (false) impression

- demonstrating *integrity* by keeping confidences and observing basic ethical guidelines to show one's concern for others

- meeting with one's employees to discuss and define exactly what is *expected* of them

- making sure that people are treated *equitably*, that is, giving equivalent rewards for similar performance by different employees and avoiding actual or apparent special treatment for favorites

- giving employees meaningful *influence* over decisions about their own work, especially how to accomplish their work goals and what to do about work problems

- adhering to clear standards that are seen as *just* and reasonable, for example, not giving praise out of proportion to accomplishments or imposing penalties disproportionate to an offense

- demonstrating *respect* toward employees, showing by actions that one really cares about others and recognizes their strengths and contributions

- following *due process*, that is, procedures that are open to public scrutiny and that permit everyone to participate actively in their application.

Many of these ten aspects of fairness relate to one of the other factors that support a TQM culture. Fairness is important for TQM because it is difficult if not impossible for employees to feel empowered, to believe that there will be rewards for results, or to act cooperatively unless they perceive conditions as fair.

One recent research study[38] showed that organizations with very positive climates of fairness are characterized by exceptionally low employee accident and sickness compensation costs. A climate of fairness can help prevent Deming's sixth and seventh deadly diseases: excessive medical costs and excessive legal liability costs. In sum, fairness is the foundation for many—perhaps most—aspects of a TQM culture.

## Culture Element 7: Equitable Compensation

Pay should be equitable across organizational levels; this means top executive pay should not be much more than about twenty times the pay of the lowest-paid full-time permanent employee.

In Japan the CEO of a typical large corporation earns ten to twenty times as much as the lowest-level salaried employee. In 1990 the average for Japanese CEOs was 17 times the wage of an ordinary worker.[39] Thus, if an assistant bookkeeper makes about $18,000, the CEO of that corporation would probably earn the equivalent of about $306,000. (In Japan year-end bonuses equal to one-third or more of a person's annual wage are common in successful firms. Thus, the actual wages might be $25,000 and $425,000; the proportions are still the same.) This is close to what experts have suggested as the optimum ratio of pay for the CEO in relation to the lowest-paid employee. Peter Drucker, for example, has argued that CEOs should earn no more than about twenty times the pay of the lowest-level employee.[40]

In most large American firms, CEOs earn from 50 to 100 times as much as the lowest-level salaried employee (85 times was the actual average for 1990).[41] Not only is executive pay in the United States higher than anywhere else in the world, it is twice as high as in the two next-highest countries, Canada and Germany.[42] Such large pay differentials make fairness more difficult to achieve and can undermine some of the other TQM culture factors. The social economist Robert B. Reich shows how financial disparities between the executive elite and other social class groups in American society have increased dramatically over the last generation and discusses the worrisome implications of this fact.[43]

It may be unrealistic to expect compensation "compression" in U.S. organizations similar to that common in Japan. Still, there is evidence that adjustments are being made to reduce the disparities in pay between executives and workers. Pressure to correct some of the more gross inequities in executive pay seems to be increasing in the United States. For example, the chairman of UAL, the parent corporation of United Airlines, earned more than $18 million in 1990, while profits fell by 71%. His pay was more than 1200 times that of a new flight attendant—and employees in that category received no pay increases at all from 1985 to 1990.

From 1980 to 1990 corporate profits rose an average of 78%, while CEO pay rose by 212%, almost triple the rate of profit increase. (Worker pay rose 58%, about two-thirds the increase in profitability.) Perhaps the greatest pressure for change is due to the widespread public reporting of CEO salaries.[44]

The capstone to the argument for limits on CEO pay is concrete evidence that when a firm's profits don't rise—and even when they go down—CEO pay still increases. Lee Iacocca received a 25% increase in total compensation in 1990, even though Chrysler's earnings decreased by 79%. The CEO of Reebok, the maker of tennis shoes, earned more than $40 million between 1988 and 1990, including 5% of pretax company profits, while the company's stock appreciated just 17%; in 1990 profit increased by 1%. In contrast, the CEO of Reebok's chief competitor, Nike, earned about $1 million over the same period. During this time Nike's return on equity was 23%. Such situations have led some firms to set caps on CEO pay.

Reebok has a new contract with its CEO limiting his cash income to a maximum of $2 million per year. But putting a limit on executive pay is not only a reaction to a negative experience. Herman Miller, a firm noted for excellence (and one we shall speak of again), instituted a policy that the CEO may not receive compensation greater than 20 times the pay of a line employee, conforming to Peter Drucker's guideline.

Even if the ratio of executive to worker pay is not altered by increasing wages at lower levels or reducing executive pay, organizations can take actions to reduce the negative effects of the disparity. Financial non-salary rewards for achievements, as we discussed earlier in this chapter, can raise employees' total compensation and thus make the top to bottom ratio more equitable. Other actions, such as employee ownership and eliminating special perks and status differences across organizational levels, can also have positive effects. Normally these latter factors emphasize pay differences. By means of various strategies, some attention can go given to the issue of gross discrepancies in pay across organizational levels.

Does all this really make any difference with respect to quality? Recent research gives a definite answer.[45] This study involved more than 100 business units in 41 different organizations in North America and Europe. These were mostly manufacturing firms, employing a total of over half a million people and with annual sales (per unit) of over $71 million. The researchers found that customers' reports of product quality were strongly related to the size of the difference between top-level and lower-level employees' pay. The smaller the difference, the higher were customers' ratings of product quality. The greater the difference, the lower were customers' quality ratings. Based on these impressive results we can reasonably conclude that equity, in terms of the size of the difference between executives' and lower-level employees' pay, is one necessary basis of a TQM culture.

---

## Culture Element 8: Employee Ownership

Employees should have an ownership stake in the organization.

In a recent best seller, CEO Harvey Mackay says, "Owning 1 percent of something is worth more than managing 100 percent of anything."[46] Research bears out Mackay's assertion. Employee-owned firms are, on the average, half again as profitable as comparable firms without some form of employee ownership.[47] In many American organizations management has discovered that employees' capitalistic economic stake in the firm seems to strengthen the other cultural factors we've been discussing. Total employee involvement becomes even more effective when workers have a stake in the firm as well as a say in work-related matters.

At Herman Miller, maker of some of the best quality office furnishings in the world, all employees *must* own company stock. Eventually the firm will be completely employee owned. In many other organizations employees become owners through an "ESOP"—employee stock ownership plan. Some such plans operate as investment retirement funds; others hold the stock in trust-like arrangements. Regardless of the structure of the plan, the common aim is to provide employees with an ownership stake.

While ownership can be a significant factor, it is not necessarily the most important factor. Of course, in some organizations, such as government agencies, publicly owned agencies, or cooperatives, employee ownership is not possible. The key is that employees must *feel* and *act* as though they are owners. Sometimes creative ways can be found to give employees a legal ownership stake. For example, the Canadian post office has publicly considered issuing stock that employees could own.[48] But even when legal ownership of the organization is impossible, employees can have a sense of ownership over their work and actions. This only happens when it is fostered by the culture created by top managers.

## Understanding TQM Culture

We have discussed eight specific elements common to TQM cultures. There are surely others, but we believe that the ones we have defined and discussed here are the most important. We have not tried to describe all cultural elements—that would probably be impossible. Our focus has been on the elements that create and maintain TQM, the ones that are crucial for TQM success.

The eight TQM culture elements are founded on certain values, the sense of what is right and what is wrong. They are based on specific beliefs about the way things work—and the way they should work—in the organization. We have tried to avoid philosophical discussions, in favor of practical specifics about the policies and practices that help define and shape culture. They do so by exhibiting, reflecting, and in concrete ways supporting the values and beliefs that underlie TQM.

Some of the eight elements are relatively simple to implement, at least in concept. Setting up an employee stock ownership plan or a policy of job security, for example, is in most organizations difficult only if management does not accept these concepts. Actually implementing an ESOP or a no-layoffs policy need not be an especially complicated undertaking.

Implementing other culture elements can be more complex and challenging. An example would be developing policies, systems, and practices that reward employees for results and for team and organizational as well as individual performance. And it can be even more difficult to make some of the elements just described a part of the organization's culture. Three obvious examples are developing a climate of fairness, instilling cooperation, and empowering employees.

In every case, however, the key is action. Leaders and managers construct and reinforce the organization's culture by their actions. Culture is created by their daily decisions and behaviors. Culture is not a mission statement that hangs on the wall. It is not a paragraph in a policy manual mentioning employee rights. It is not an isolated event in the company's history. It does not mean treating employees to a Christmas luncheon once a year. What, then *is* culture?

*Culture is the cumulative perception of how the organization treats people and how people expect to treat one another. It is based on consistent and persistent management action, as seen by employees, vendors, and customers.*[49]

Virginia Fibre Corporation has been working to improve its TQM culture ever since the company was founded more than fifteen years ago. Its president, Charlie Chandler, recently said of VFC employees and the culture they have created, "We have a special relationship where we can talk about anything within the company and the future of the company. . . . I can't imagine going back to where . . . there are sharks swimming down the hallway—each department trying to get one up on the other."

Only by actively implementing the eight TQM culture elements described in this chapter is the foundation of a TQM culture developed. The greatest difficulty is making a continuing, long-term commitment to TQM. Virginia Fibre has been at it for fifteen years. In the next chapter we will examine some of the ways this long-term commitment comes about.

## Endnotes

1.  Reported by Aaron Bernstein, "How to Motivate Workers: Don't Watch 'Em," *Business Week*, April 29, 1991, p. 56.

2.  See the work cited in note 1.

3.  See Kathleen D. Ryan and Daniel K. Oestreich, *Driving Fear Out of the Workplace* (San Francisco: Jossey-Bass, 1991).

4.  This and some of the examples that follow are reported in two articles written for the Associated Press by Sharon Cohen that appeared in many American newspapers during the week of December 24, 1990. The articles can be found, for example, in the Memphis, Tennessee, *Commercial Appeal* of December 25 and 26, 1990, on pp. B10–B11 and B4–B5, respectively.

5.  For a detailed description of this organization and how its owner and chief executive went about changing its culture, see Ralph Strayer's article "How I Learned to Let My Workers Lead" (*Harvard Business Review*, November/December, 1990, pp. 66–69 and following).

6.  For current as well as classic readings on the subject of self-managing teams, see Rollin Glaser (Ed.), *Classic Readings in Self-Managing Teamwork* (King of Prussia, PA: Organization Design and Development, 1992).

7.  Tom Peters, *Thriving on Chaos: Handbook for a Management Revolution* (New York: Knopf, 1988), p. 292.

8.  See the work cited in note 7.

9.  These examples are detailed by Ralph Strayer in the article cited in note 5.

10. Arnold S. Tannenbaum (Ed.), *Control in Organizations* (New York: McGraw-Hill, 1968).

11. In personal communication, Jon Bird, who has extensive personal and business experience in Japan, points out to us that most Japanese organizations the twice-yearly bonus payment does not

depend very much on company performance. The difference between bonus payments in a good and a bad year, he says, is almost never more than 10%. In Japan, in most firms, bonus payments relate only marginally to performance. Their real function, says Bird, is to remove four to six months of earnings from the regular payroll. This reduces retirement payments, which are based on "regular" twelve-month earnings, not including bonuses. The system, observes Bird, "actually lowers corporate retirement costs while still providing some motivation to the Japanese worker."

12.    A comprehensive review of the major gainsharing systems used by American firms, including Fein's "Improshare," the Scanlon Plan, and others can be found in Brian Graham-Moore and Timothy L. Ross, *Gainsharing: Plans for Improving Performance* (Washington, DC: BNA Books, 1990). Basic descriptions of two of the most commonly used plans, Improshare and the Scanlon Plan, can also be found in these two "classic" references: Frederick G. Lesieur and Elbridge S. Puckett, "The Scanlon Plan Has Proved Itself" (*Harvard Business Review*, September/October 1969, pp. 109–118), and Mitchell Fein, "Improving Productivity by Improved Sharing" (*Conference Board Record*, July 1976, pp. 44–49).

13.    See the work cited in note 7, p. 30.

14.    This information from an interview conducted by Garry Coleman, of the Virginia Productivity Center, with Charlie Chandler, CEO of VFC.

15.    According to Don Dewar, a well-known quality control consultant, cited in *Sales and Marketing Management* and later quoted in the March 15, 1991, issue of the newsletter *Boardroom Reports*.

16.    William H. Davidson, "Small-Group Activity at Musashi Semiconductor Works," *Sloan Management Review*, Spring 1982, pp. 3–14.

17.    Geert Hofstede, "Motivation, Leadership, and Organization: Do American Theories Apply Abroad?" *Organizational Dynamics*, Summer 1980, pp. 42–62.

18.    Bob Stoltz, program supervisor, in *Employee Benefit News*, cited in *Boardroom Reports*, August 1, 1992, p. 8.

19.  Eugene K. Johnson, *Total Quality Management and Performance Appraisal: To Be or Not to Be? A Literature Review and Case Studies* (Washington, DC: Research and Demonstration Division, U.S. Office of Personnel Management, 1990).

20.  Quoted in an interview in the *Wall Street Journal*, June 1, 1990.

21.  Peter R. Scholtes, "An Elaboration on Deming's Teachings on Performance Appraisal." In G. N. McLean, S. R. Damme, and R. A. Swanson (Eds.), *Performance Appraisal: Perspectives on a Quality Management Approach* (Alexandria, VA: American Society for Training and Development, 1990).

22.  Richard E. Walton, "From Control to Commitment in the Workplace," *Harvard Business Review*, March/April 1985, pp. 76–84.

23.  Quoted in an interview, "Talking business with Juran of the Juran Institute," in the *New York Times*, February 6, 1990, p. D2.

24.  Quoted by Sharon Cohen. See the work cited in note 4.

25.  See the work cited in note 22.

26.  See, for example, Alfie Kohn's book *No Contest: The Case Against Competition* (Boston: Houghton Mifflin, 1988).

27.  See the work by Alfie Kohn cited in note 25 and Rafael Aguayo, *Dr. Deming: The American Who Taught the Japanese About Quality* (New York: Carol Publishing Group, 1990).

28.  Reported in the *Washington Post*, July 4, 1991, pp. A1, A28.

29.  Peter F. Drucker, "Don't Change Corporate Culture—Use It!" *Wall Street Journal*, March 28, 1992, Editorial page.

30.  For a good example, see David Halberstam's description of the Japanese recovery after World War II in his book *The Reckoning* (New York: William Morrow, 1986).

31.  Interview with Louise Kehoe and Geoffrey Owen in the *Financial Times*, July 3, 1992.

32.  Deming sees driving out fear as an especially important aspect of his philosophy of management, emphasizing it as the eighth of his

fourteen points. For further details, see the work by Kathleen D. Ryan and Daniel K. Oestreich cited in note 3.

33.   For a detailed discussion, see William T. Morris, *Work and Your Future* (Englewood Cliffs, NJ: Reston Publishing Co./a Prentice-Hall company, 1975, pp. 118–123).

34.   These and other issues centered on the fallacy of cost reduction as a strategy for increasing profit are considered by Rafael Aguayo in the first two chapters of the work cited in note 26.

35.   Jeffrey J. Mayer, *If You Don't Have the Time to Do It Right the First Time, When Will You Find the Time to Do It Over?* (New York: Simon & Schuster, 1990).

36.   From the brochure of Greenfield Associates, a licensee of the well-known consulting firm Wilson Learning Corporation.

37.   Frederick R. Reichheld and W. Earl Sasser, Jr., "Zero Defections: Quality Comes to Services," *Harvard Business Review*, September/October, 1990, pp. 105–114.

38.   Marshall Sashkin and Richard L. Williams, "Does Fairness Make a Difference? *Organizational Dynamics*, Autumn 1990, pp. 56–71.

39.   John A. Byrne, "The Flap Over Executive Pay," *Business Week*, May 6, 1991, p. 95.

40.   See the work cited in note 38.

41.   See the work cited in note 38, p. 96.

42.   Louis Uchitelle, "No Recession for Executive Pay," *New York Times*, March 18, 1991, pp. C1, C4

43.   Robert B. Reich, *The Work of Nations* (New York: Knopf, 1991).

44.   The information and examples cited here were reported in a cover story in *Business Week*, May 6, 1991, pp. 95–112. For more details, see Graef Crystal, *In Search of Excess* (New York: Norton, 1992).

45.   Douglas M. Cowherd and David I. Levine, "Product Quality and Pay Equity between Lower-level Employees and Top Management: An

Investigation of Distributive Justice Theory." *Administration Times Quarterly,* June 1, 1992, 37, pp. 302–320.

46.    Harvey Mackay, *Swim with the Sharks Without Being Eaten Alive* (New York: William Morrow, 1988, p. 191).

47.    Michael Conte and Arnold S. Tannenbaum, *Employee Ownership* (Ann Arbor: Survey Research Center, Institute for Social Research, University of Michigan, 1980).

48.    Richard L. Williams helped draft this discussion of the nature of culture.

49.    John Urquhart, "Canada May Let Mail Workers Buy Shares in Agency," *Wall Street Journal,* May 1, 1992.

# 6

# Creating and Supporting a TQM Culture

Many of the culture elements defined in Chapter Five are implemented through organizational policies, plans, programs, and practices. In Chapter Three we discussed the statistical tools for applying TQM. Similarly, we think of the methods for constructing or changing organizational culture as "social" tools for developing TQM. Just as the seven old tools build quality through statistical process control, the social tools can build the culture needed to support long-term TQM. Like the statistical tools, some social tools are relatively simple and easy to apply, while others are much more difficult to use and require considerable skill. We will look at some of these social tools, their use, and their effects.

Even the simpler social tools call for a degree of skill and knowledge. The more complex social tools require leadership, visionary leadership. Top executives must act as leaders and become culture builders. These are the difficult issues we will explore by examining the nature of cultural leadership and the ways in which visionary leaders build TQM cultures.

## Social Tools to Develop Cultural Values

The social tools—management policies, plans, programs, and practices—establish and support the eight culture elements and the values that are at the heart of these elements. We will describe several of these social tools and examine how they relate to certain of the eight elements of a TQM culture.

### Empowering Through Job Design

Sometimes called *job redesign* or *job enrichment,* job design usually defines (or redefines) tasks so that the work activities of an employee (or team) make up a "whole" job.[1] That is, job design aims to create tasks that are coherent and complete, that provide people with a feeling of accomplishment. Good job design also gives employees greater control over their work actions. Control over decisions about how to do the job and how to solve work-related problems is especially important. It generally means that authority is commensurate with responsibility. *Empowerment* is the social science jargon term most often used to refer to this aim.

Some scholars suggest that empowerment necessarily involves a certain set of conditions.[2] These conditions include aspects of job design along with some other factors that we discussed in Chapter Five. First, workers must believe that their work efforts can result in positive outcomes. People must also feel competent and able to do their work effectively. Earlier, we referred to enabling conditions. This implies mastery of the knowledge, skills, and actions required to do one's job, what we've called *enablement.* Finally, employees must have the authority to make work-related decisions. Such control must be designed into the job.

An early job design study carried out in Great Britain involved sales representatives.[3] The study was planned as a formal experiment. One group of employees had their jobs changed in certain respects while another "control group" of sales reps continued doing the job the old way. Reps in the experimental group were, for example, given authority to determine the frequency with which they visited customers. Previously, reps had to have their managers approve their sales visit schedules. Now, the reps were the only ones who kept and saw these records. This is consistent with our discussion of the first TQM culture element: Information must be used for quality improvement, not to control employees. Sales reps were also given authority to settle customer complaints involving up to $250 on the spot. They could agree to accept return of faulty or surplus materials, even if the materials were old and obsolete. Reps also had authority to negotiate prices and give discounts.

Fifteen sales representatives were in the experimental group, while another 23 served as the control. Those in the control group did their jobs the old way. Neither group had an economic advantage, such as the biggest customers or the best-selling product line. Moreover, during the previous year the average performance for sales reps in the two groups was about the same. The test was to compare sales during the experimental period with sales during the same period of the previous year.

After nine months, sales for reps in the control group had declined about 5% on the average. In contrast, sales reps in the experimental group increased their gross revenues by about 19% over the previous year. This increase represented more than $300,000 in sales. In terms of performance, the job design clearly paid off. How about employees' satisfaction with the changes? Reps in the control group were neither more nor less satisfied after the study. But reps in the experimental group reported that they enjoyed their work more than they had in the past.

### Designing Complete Jobs

To support TQM, work must be designed to form a coherent whole job that is intrinsically meaningful. Considerable psychological research shows that people strive for a sense of completion, not just in work but in general.[4]

Another study shows how both control and coherence can become a natural part of the job. This research focused on the assembly of washing machine water pumps. The job was done on an assembly line basis by six operators, each of whom added certain parts to the pump chassis. This was changed so that a single person assembled an entire pump. Besides having a more complete job, workers could now control their own work pace. Employees were also responsible for inspecting and approving the finished pump. The result was shorter assembly time, improved quality, and reduced cost.[5]

### Design for Teamwork

Herzberg's original approach to job enrichment was centered on the individual worker.[6] He believed that whole jobs over which people had more complete control would be intrinsically more motivating, leading employees to produce more with increased quality. While there is some truth to this notion, it is also incomplete. Individuals can, without too much difficulty, master the skills needed to carry out all the operations in producing a washing machine water pump.

But today's manufacturing and service work presents many new and complex technical problems. Solving those problems calls for more knowledge and skill than most individuals can be reasonably expected to possess. And it's often important to take action on the spot. Only teams are likely to have the resources needed to deal quickly and effectively with technically complex problems. The issue here is not simply motivation. Work must be designed so that the necessary knowledge and skill resources are there.

Good job design does even more than empower employees by giving them control over their own actions and a sense of achievement from completing a whole job. When job design is carried out properly, it also provides for team-based cooperative interactions with others.[7] Team-based job design is especially important, since it supports cooperation, makes team rewards possible, and helps foster a climate of fairness.

Soon after Herzberg's pioneering work had become popular, others began to apply job enrichment to team operations, not just to design or redesign individuals' jobs. In Europe, a major electronics manufacturer, Phillips, redesigned the assembly operations in a factory that produced color television sets. The assembly line was broken into shorter, team-operated segments. Every team produced a complete subassembly, a major whole part of the final product. Both productivity and quality improved.

The classic U.S. example of team-based work design is that of a pet food factory in Topeka, Kansas.[8] The plant was designed new from the ground up, and employees were to have much greater authority than in traditionally designed plants. They also had the skill to do many different parts of a job, and the work was to be done by self-managing teams of seven to fourteen employees, with no first-line supervisors. Teams not only worked as a unit, they solved problems as a group, distributed the work, made operating decisions, and even interviewed and hired new team members.

Although the plant's performance was outstanding from the start, it took a relatively long time for the plant to become the model for the entire organization that top managers had planned. In part, the plant was so effective that it made other, older plants look bad. Managers were literally shunned by those in the other plants. The successful managers in this new plant were blocked from promotions to other plants. Some saw their careers deadended. Top-level managers in older plants didn't want to reward a new approach that made their own plants seem ineffective.

When two organizational cultures collide, the one that survives may not be the one that is most effective and functional. Other major team-based redesign efforts, both in Europe and the United States, have failed when the culture of the larger system overwhelms the part of the system involved in the change. Persistence and the continuing support of top management can, however, lead to long-term success. Fortunately, in the case of the pet food factory, top management remained committed to the new plant concept, and over the long haul it became accepted and copied.

"Self-managing teams" have become very popular in the past few years.[9] The approach derives in part from the sort of "socio-technical system design" experiments just discussed. But its popularity does not mean that companies rush to copy interesting experiments. The increasing use of this sort of team work design is based on evidence that autonomous teams, with whole jobs and authority equal to responsibility, are a more effective and less costly way to get the job done.[10]

Levi Strauss & Co. is in the process of converting its 27 U.S. plants to team operations. One reason is to show that through teamwork American plant can compete economically with over-seas operations. In the first plant to change over completely to teams, in the spring of 1992, defects were reduced by 25% as compared with the same time period of the previous year.[11]

Throughout our discussion of TQM, we have emphasized the importance of teamwork. TQM tools and techniques are, for the most part, designed to be used by teams. Teams are better able than individuals to define, collect, and use information for improvement. Teams are also the most important focus for the design of operations so that quality can be built in at the five checkpoints described in Chapter Four. Finally, teams support several of the values and beliefs that are required for a TQM culture, especially the value of cooperation.

### Using Job Design for TQM

The preceding examples, and hundreds of others, show that effective job design fulfills three basic adult human work needs:[12]

- the need for control over one's actions[13]

- the need for achievement through accomplishment of com-plete tasks[14]

- the need for work-relevant interaction with others[15]

These three factors are the essence of participative management. They are what make participative management work.[16] There are many approaches to job design, but they are all variations on the same basic themes: increased control, more meaningful and complete activities, and team-based interaction.

It is probably something of an oversimplification to speak of job design as if it were a single, specific tool. Even so, as a general approach, job design is one of the best known and most widely used tools for building a TQM culture. Recall the eight culture elements we defined earlier. As described here, job design makes authority equal to responsibility (Element 2). It instills coopera- tion and teamwork (Element 4). Job design supports a policy of rewards for results (Element 3) and is consistent with the appropriate use of quality measurement (Element 1). In sum, job design can have an important positive effect on several of the eight TQM culture elements. It is an important tool for building a TQM culture.

### Encouraging Employee Ownership

In Chapter Five we mentioned several employee ownership programs (such as ESOPs and individual stock purchase options). Of the eight culture elements that we identified, employee ownership, while useful and potentially powerful in impact, is probably the least crucial for TQM. Some researchers and managers used to think that employee ownership motivates employees and leads to positive effects from participative employee involvement. More recent research, however, suggests that the opposite is true.

A major research study involving 45 firms with some form of employee ownership concluded that employee ownership plans lead to high satisfaction and outstanding organizational perfor- mance when employees have "participative opportunities on the job."[17] Similar findings were obtained in an earlier research study involving three firms in the northeastern United States and western Canada.[18]

Only when employee empowerment and participation exist does employee ownership appear to have a strong positive effect. It may be that empowerment and participation work on a real-time basis to show employees that ownership can have direct and tangible effects.

### Ensuring Fair Pay for Performance

Pay policies directly affect three of the culture elements: rewards for results, fairness (that is, equity of rewards), and equitable compensation. In Chapter Five we raised the issue of unfairness when discussing extreme disparities in pay across organizational levels. And we noted that the latest research results are striking in demonstrating the strong relationship between high quality, as seen by customers, and small pay disparity from top to bottom organization levels.[19] However, the most obvious solution, compensation compression, is difficult to act on. Most American firms are unlikely to adopt a more equitable, let alone egalitarian, pay approach just because the Japanese do it. Compensation compression can have a profound positive effect, showing employees in a dramatic way the basic fairness of management. Still, while important, it is probably not a necessary condition for a TQM culture in most American organizations.

That is, "equitable" pay does not mean "equal" pay. Many people incorrectly assume that equality is the same as equity. Equity, which is crucial for TQM, means that people agree that rewards (or punishments) are allocated in the same way to everyone. For example, if one person's job is twice as hard as another's, it would be equitable for the first person to be paid twice as much. So, even though some people receive greater rewards than others, the situation is equitable if it is generally agreed that those individuals have acted in ways that demonstrate their unequal rewards are deserved. A completely equitable system can easily result in very unequal allocation of rewards, because equitable rewards are based on the value that one's actions, activities, and products add to the organization.

American culture supports strongly the right of an individual to "rise to the top" and achieve great rewards. It is not important or even appropriate for management to try to make all employees' compensation equal. What is crucial is that management makes sure pay is equitable (fair) and that everyone is aware of this. It is, in fact, essential that managers show—by their actions—that an underlying climate of fairness, of equity, exists. This applies to each of the ten dimensions of fairness defined in Chapter Five.

We have discussed two important ways to demonstrate equity: rewarding results through a formal profit-sharing or gainsharing plan and fostering employee ownership. Programs and policies that strengthen these culture elements will at the same time reduce the negative effect of a relatively large spread in pay between lower and upper organizational levels.

### Guaranteeing Secure Jobs

Ensuring job security is a direct, positive response to Deming's injunction to drive out fear. We noted earlier that a surprising number of the best U.S. organizations have formal job security policies. Some have had them for many years. It was in 1923 that William C. Procter, then president of Procter & Gamble, *guaranteed* workers 48 weeks of employment a year.[20] Even so, many organizations still resist adopting such policies. This is unfortunate; guaranteed job security is a policy that can benefit the organization as much as it does employees.

Rafael Aguayo contrasts the responses of Chrysler and Mazda when each faced financial difficulties. At Chrysler, CEO Lynn Townsend fired many engineers. Costs were dramatically reduced and the balance sheet improved—in the short run. But soon the firm was in even worse shape. It required massive infusions of funds borrowed from the federal government to save Chrysler. At Mazda, not a single engineer was laid off. However, many were given new assignments, including work as salesmen in dealer showrooms. When conditions improved a few years later, the engineers who had been assigned to sales returned with incredibly valuable new insights into customers' needs. They could apply their learnings directly to design and engineering activities. While Chrysler was asking for protection and federal loans, Mazda was experiencing a boom.[21]

Rubbermaid Corporation, in Wooster, Ohio, tells employees that the reward for productivity is job security. The fact is, however, that job security is, in the long run, the best way to ensure productivity! Providing employees with secure jobs may be the most convincing evidence of management's commitment to TQM.

## Creating a Climate of Fairness

The concept of fairness incorporates and reflects many of the culture elements identified in Chapter Five. Implementing this concept is not easy, but neither is it impossible. The aim is not sainthood but effective management behavior. Managers must examine their behaviors, the ones shown to relate to the various dimensions of fairness (equity, consistency, fair procedures, and so on). They benefit especially from individual, personalized feedback that shows exactly how others see their actions. This sort of reality test enables managers to see their actions more clearly and accurately than ever before. With coaching and trained assistance, managers can then make specific changes. Only by changing their behavior, by altering actions that employees see as unfair, can managers create an organizational climate of fairness.[22]

## The Impact of Social Tools

We have described some commonly used social/organizational tools. Some of those mentioned are especially important. We included some others because of their widespread use. However, our aim was to provide examples, not to make a comprehensive list of the available social tools. Moreover, when selecting examples we purposely chose tools targeting one or another of the eight culture elements. Each of the eight is directly affected by one or more of our examples.

Some of the social tools that we have discussed—job design, participative management (authority equal to responsibility), and employee ownership, for example—have been and are still being used as organizational programs apart from TQM. None, however, provides a dramatic quick fix to organizational problems.[23] Just as Deming points out the folly of trying to pick and choose which of his fourteen points to use, we can say that it is not enough to implement one or another favorite social tool. Research shows that the benefits are greater when programs such as participation and employee ownership are combined.[24] The more extensive and consistent the efforts to change culture are, the greater the impact. And the more these efforts contribute to the development of a culture that defines and supports TQM, the better and the longer-lasting the effects.

Job design and the other policies, plans, programs, and practices that we discussed are some of the many social tools that can be used to define organizational climate and culture. These tools may seem "soft" at first glance, but this is not true. They represent major changes in the way managers think and act, as does TQM. In that sense, they are quite "hard" and—sometimes—hard to apply.

Culture, the set of shared beliefs and values that define and direct human behavior in social systems, is created and shaped only by consistent patterns of action. And those action patterns must be carried out over long periods of time. Policies, plans, programs, and procedures can all help define values and beliefs and guide managers in their efforts to make those values and beliefs part of the organization's culture. But in the end only practices—actions—count. Neither wall plaques nor positions espoused by top management, no matter how loudly, convincingly, or often, can define or instill values and beliefs. TQM will flourish only when there is alignment between what top managers preach and what they practice, as seen by people throughout the organization.

Defining a philosophy that embodies a vision and then ensuring that it is reflected in action are the tasks of leadership. Social tools are useful only in the context of culture-building leadership.

## Constructing Culture Through Leadership

In the early 1980s Terrence Deal and Alan Kennedy pioneered in the study of what they called *corporate cultures*.[25] They showed how to "read" the culture by looking for symbols and attending to formal and informal activities. These activities—rituals, ceremonies, and traditions, for example—reflect underlying values and beliefs. The stories and "legends" that people tell, even the gossip one overhears, can help uncover and understand an organization's culture.

It was tempting to some to skip directly from expressions of culture to the shaping of culture. Some consultants suggested that managers could shape culture by constructing traditions and ceremonies, by engaging in rituals, and by telling stories that illustrated the values they wanted to "embed" in the organization's culture.[26] But *shaping* culture is very different from *expressing* culture. One organizational psychologist who has studied organizational cultures for years points out that ceremonies, traditions, and other cultural expressions can help clarify and reinforce certain values and beliefs. He adds, however, that these activities probably cannot define those values and beliefs or instill them within the organization.[27] At worst, when overt cultural symbols contradict the values and beliefs that are at work in the organization, management is tarred with the brush of hypocrisy.

In Chapter Five we identified some elements of culture that must be present to support TQM. Such policies as "no layoffs" and programs such as job design help support these TQM culture elements. It is difficult to explain how to use these and other social tools to construct cultural elements, to make changes and make them stick. And, hard as it may be to implement the programs and policies that support TQM, this is *not* the first or the most important step in creating a TQM culture.

More recently, Deal and others have identified several strategic leadership actions. These actions define values and beliefs and make them a part of the organization's culture.[28] It is employees' direct experience of the patterns of management behavior and action that defines the values and beliefs that make up the culture, not management-orchestrated symbolism. It is consistent management action, over time, that constructs culture. This is not usually easy but, when it happens, it can create cultures that are very stable—and very hard to change.

A consultant was hired by a Fortune 500 manufacturer.[29] The consultant was asked to help with a plant that had a history of poor labor relations and low productivity. Central headquarters sent him in to study the plant and its operations without giving plant management advance warning. He interviewed various employees, who told him about Sam, the plant manager. Sam was as big as a gorilla and had a temper much worse. Sam had once taken a sledgehammer and personally demolished a product he didn't like the looks of. Another time he drove his car into the plant, climbed on the roof, and screamed at the workers.

The consultant was horrified but assumed he now knew the cause of the plant's problems. He screwed up his courage and went to see the plant manager. Behind the desk was an ordinary-looking fellow named Paul. Asked where Sam was, Paul said, "Sam's been dead for nine years." Paul and the consultant spent four years undoing Sam's cultural legacy.

Leadership from the very top is what drives TQM. Only when organizational executives—especially the CEO—are absolutely committed to TQM is there a chance for long-term success. One TQM consultant has observed that while some localized improvements may be possible without top-level commitment, TQM cannot be achieved otherwise.[30] Only through leadership can the values that we have defined and discussed become part of the organization's culture. This is another reason why Deming's deadly disease of management job-hopping is so malignant. Constant turnover at the top of the organization means that leaders never have the time needed to build a TQM culture.

It may seem that we overemphasize leadership at the expense of action at lower levels. This is not so; action involvement on the part of lower-level employees is the essence of TQM. No number of special cross-area quality task force groups making presentations to top managers will create a TQM organization. No pronouncements from a top-level quality council will make TQM work. Neither will anything done by top-level leaders if the people doing the work of the organization are not deeply and directly involved in applying TQM in the context of their normal work activities.

Top-level leadership is crucial for TQM, but so is lower-level support and action. It is, then, something of a paradox yet absolutely true that the way TQM really works is top-down from the bottom up. As Deming says, it is the role of management to define and design the system and to do so in a way that builds in quality. In a traditional organization, employees are responsible only for operating the system, but they often don't have the authority they need to do so effectively. TQM organizations are designed so that employees have the authority needed to carry out their responsibilities effectively. But TQM goes even further. Employees are the primary force for continuously improving the system. They are involved in constantly revising, refining, even redesigning work processes throughout the organization to maintain and improve quality.

In operation TQM depends on the efforts of those who do the core work of the organization, although Deming is correct when he says that everyone must take action to accomplish the transformation. Still, it is leadership that sets these processes in motion. Leaders bring people together under a shared vision. They create the conditions under which that vision can be made real.

They do this by constructing an organizational culture based on the values and beliefs that define and support TQM.

## How Do Leaders Construct Cultures?

In his wonderful book *Leadership Is an Art*, CEO Max De Pree says, "The first responsibility of a leader is to define reality. The last is to say thank you. In between the two, the leader must become a servant and a debtor."[31] He goes on to explain, almost poetically, how leaders define reality and what they do next. We will cite some examples of De Pree's images of leadership as we try to explain just what leaders do, as servants and debtors, to define organizational reality by constructing a culture.

There are three primary types of strategic action that leaders use, more or less in sequence, to construct organizational cultures. First, leaders define a value-based organizational philosophy. Next, they create policies and set up programs based on the philosophy. This is where many of the eight culture elements that support TQM come into play. Finally (really, all along), they model cultural values and beliefs through their constant and consistent behavior. This may sound like a simple set of 1-2-3 actions, but it is not. It is the most difficult and complicated set of undertakings related to organizations. We will consider in more detail the nature of each of the three types of strategic action.

### Defining an Organizational Philosophy

Leaders start with a value-based vision of what the organization should be. This vision explicitly includes TQM values and beliefs. Shaping this vision requires a level of cognitive capability that is uncommon if not rare. The leader must work with top executives to identify in clear and simple terms just what the organization is about. The office furniture manufacturer Herman Miller was founded in 1923 by Max De Pree's father. From the beginning, a shared philosophy and values were important. Seventy years of culture building are reflected in Max De Pree's book, which is essentially a statement of the company philosophy and values. In it, he writes that candidates for senior executive positions "should understand and speak for the corporate value system."[32]

Leaders are not, however, in the business of selling their personal visions and values. In fact, they rely on others to help identify the essential elements of the vision and values that become the organization's philosophy. They depend especially on other executives, but they include others at all organizational levels. When there is a union, top union officials also participate in developing this consensus on organizational values and vision. The process of defining an organizational philosophy is one of creating a *shared* vision.

If working with top executives to discuss and define a shared vision seems like a straightforward assignment, consider this description of one such effort by the CEO involved:

> We spent three days. . . . Around the table sat our chief oper-
> ating officer, the executive vice-president of corporate market-
> ing and development, the vice-president of administration, and
> me. . . . We sat there hour after hour in an intense debate about
> the company. We simply could not agree on what Consumers
> Packaging was and is, never mind what it should be in the
> future. . . . Here was a group of executives who had been with
> Consumers for a total of ninety-one years—four people who, I
> thought, really knew the company. *We didn't have a common
> language or any way to proceed.*[33] [Emphasis added.]

One reason this group found its task so difficult was that its members jumped into the process of defining a new culture without first looking at where the organization had been and where it then stood. In order to change an organization's culture, to construct a new one, or to simply renew the culture by reemphasizing existing but latent values and beliefs, top managers must begin by reading the existing culture, including its history and current status. A new or changed culture does not suddenly appear out of a vacuum. Cultures are deeply affected by past and present circumstances; it is foolish to think that one can design a new culture while ignoring the past and the present.

In another case, the difficult process of defining the organization's values and philosophy was completed, but the new philosophy did not seem to take. The cause was opposition, both subtle and overt, from a key senior manager who could not give up the old ways. Only after removing this individual from the position of authority in which he could block the executive group's strategy was true consensus achieved. Only then could the group implement a new organizational vision and philosophy.[34]

### Creating Policies and Implementing Programs

Once they have developed consensus among top managers on the values and vision, leaders define policies and approve specific programs like the ones we described in the preceding chapter. These policies and programs support TQM philosophy and action. The best policies and programs create patterns of action that support TQM. Through policies and programs, TQM values become part of organizational action in the day-to-day operation of the firm.

An organizational policy is a statement, usually public and in writing, that tells how the philosophy applies to a specific organizational practice, such as staffing, purchasing, or dealing with customer problems. For example, most organizations have staffing policies that emphasize examination of job candidates' academic or skill qualifications and require candidates to complete various personnel tests. In contrast, an organization involved in TQM might have a staffing policy stating that hiring decisions must take into account the extent to which candidates exhibit through their past actions the values crucial to the organization's philosophy.

Many organizations have purchasing policies that require them to select the lowest of three bids. An organization applying

TQM might instead have a purchasing policy that defines the parameters under which employees are expected to make purchase decisions without higher-level approval, thus explicitly supporting their empowerment in this respect. It is not unusual for organizations to have a merchandise return or service adjustment policy that requires management review of customer documents and customer service staff recommendations before approving an adjustment. For TQM, a policy centered on customer problems might state that customer service staff have full authority to make whatever adjustment they decide is appropriate, based on the company's commitment to quality for the customer.

Policies that define how rewards are to be allocated are especially important for constructing culture. At Herman Miller, CEO Max De Pree instituted a policy that the maximum salary could be no more than twenty times the salary of the lowest-level full-time permanent employee. This policy supports several of the TQM culture elements discussed in Chapter Five. Another crucial policy area is staffing, particularly the hiring of key staff members. Leaders engaged in constructing organizational cultures take great care to select senior staff whose values and beliefs are similar to or consistent with those the leader is trying to inculcate.

In a conversation with one of the authors a CEO explained how he had instituted exciting new ceremonies in the organization. His intent was to strengthen the organization's culture, as he had been taught in an executive development program. "What," he was asked, "were your first important actions when you became CEO?" Without hesitation he replied, "Why the first thing I did was to bring on board a few key people who I really knew and could rely on." That is, the CEO chose people whose values and beliefs fit with his own and who would support his long-term plans for shaping the organization's culture.

Of course, we don't mean to suggest that to change cultures CEOs always begin by replacing top managers. Often, individuals with supportive values will be found within the organization, if not in key positions. Our point is that leaders who build cultures look for such individuals, both inside and outside the organization. Such persons help support the organizational values, philosophy, and vision that the leader is trying to define and instill. Ceremonies and other symbols *reinforce* culture. Important task- and goal-relevant actions, like hiring key staff, *shape* culture.

This is not to say that symbolic factors should be forgotten; quite the reverse. It is important for policies and programs to incorporate symbolic activities—rituals, ceremonies, and so forth. Symbols reinforce both values and actions that relate to policies and programs. Consider, for example, a ceremony to present a team with a customer satisfaction achievement award along with a cash bonus for the team members. The symbolic activity adds an intangible meaning to the tangible reward. It strengthens the policy or program, which is now more visible and real. What's more, the symbolic activity reinforces the values behind the policy. Equity, rewards for results, and authority equal to responsibility are just a few of the values demonstrated by the team' actions and highlighted by the symbolic recognition. It is always important to link tangible work actions and outcomes with intangible symbols and meanings. This is how culture is constructed.

A program usually refers to a special, planned set of activities, sometimes with a starting and an ending date. Programs, like policies, put the organization's philosophy and the values that define that philosophy into action. There might, for example, be a special program to train employees to collect information to assess customer problems and make data-based decisions about corrective actions. Such a program could be important if the TQM-based customer-problem policy that we mentioned earlier is to work well. Programs often support or put certain policies into action. And both policies and programs express the values on which the organization's philosophy is based.

Many of the TQM culture elements that we defined can be supported by specific programs and policies. Policies and programs follow the development of an organizational philosophy and vision. They follow because their consistency with the values defined in the philosophy and their contribution to the attainment of the vision must be tested. It is through policies and programs that abstractions such as values, beliefs, and vision come into contact with organizational reality.

### Modeling Values and Beliefs Through Leadership Behavior

Leaders engage in personal actions that illustrate and reinforce TQM values. This modeling is just as important as defining values and making sure they are reflected in organizational actions. Through these personal actions leaders demonstrate a constancy of purpose. They show their commitment to achieving the organizational vision of total quality management.

The CEO of a very large retailing conglomerate was touring a store encumbered by the usual retinue of vice-presidents, regional and local officials, and miscellaneous attendants. In the midst of a briefing by a vice-president, the CEO noticed a customer wandering down an aisle. He said, "Excuse me for a moment" to the vice-president and walked over to the customer. "Is there something you can't find that I might help you with?" the CEO asked. By his action the CEO strengthened the value of service to the customer more than any policy memorandum ever could. In fact, the value probably received more support from this CEO's action than from a year's worth of customer service training.

A recent study of school principals provides another illustration of how leaders define reality and inculcate values by their behavior. The Experience Sampling Study was conducted at the National Center for Research and Development on School Leadership at the University of Illinois. Seventy-five principals wore electronic pagers (beepers) for a week. The beepers went off at random; each time, the principal was to write on a card what he or she was doing. At 3:15 P.M. one day the beepers all went off. One principal wrote, "Supervising school bus loading." Across town another wrote, "Encouraging kids to have high achievement goals (as they get on buses)." One principal was acting, quite properly, to manage the school organization. The other was, through her actions, exhibiting the values that support TQM.

Max De Pree tells about a group meeting to discuss a new inventory program.[35] An employee asked him if he understood the program and was committed to it. He said that he didn't understand it fully but was committed. The employee thought this odd. De Pree asked about her job and how things were going in her department. She said things were just fine. He asked if he "should be comfortable about what was going on" in her department. She said he could. Was she comfortable about the way he was doing his job? De Pree then asked. At this point, the employee got the message, responding that she was, even though she didn't understand everything he did. The point De Pree was trying to make was that even though we don't, and can't, fully understand what everyone else does, we can be committed to one another and can trust one another. In this exchange, De Pree illustrated what he calls "an essential value," the value of trusting "one another to be accountable for our own assignments."

### What Leaders Do

Peter Senge is well known for his work regarding the "learning organization" and the disciplines required to create learning organizations.[36] But in a less well-known article, Senge describes in some detail the sort of leadership required in learning organizations.[37] He defines three roles of the leader. First, the leader must be a *designer*. That is, the leader must help define a vision, an organizational philosophy, and show how this design can be built into the organization's strategic operations and its culture. Doing this, making the design come alive, is part of the leader's role as *steward*. De Pree, too, speaks of the leader as steward and servant. Senge explains that this refers to the leader's role in empowering others to act to achieve organizational aims, to make real a shared vision by applying the philosophy embodying that vision. Finally, Senge identifies the role of the leader as *teacher*. Leaders teach primarily by acting as models, illustrating by their own behavior the values and beliefs central to the organization's design. In this way, leaders show that others, too, can by their own actions help implement the organizational design.

Of course, Senge's three roles closely parallel the three strategies just described: defining shared values and developing an organizational philosophy (designer), creating policies and programs that empower people (steward), and modeling values (teacher). The convergence of Senge's views with our own suggests that we are all on the right track in beginning to understand how leaders build culture.

## What About the Union?

We noted, in passing, that when there is a union its senior officers must participate in developing the organizational philosophy. They must work along with the CEO and top managers to define values and a vision. This is easy to say but difficult to accomplish, and it is getting harder.

George Kourpias, president of the International Association of Machinists (IAM), issued a "white paper" in the fall of 1990, setting forth the union's views regarding TQM. He states that "it is the policy of the IAM to oppose team concept proposals." He refers in particular to what the IAM calls "the Deming system." In a letter to union officers Kourpias wrote, "These programs by their very nature interfere with our duty to protect the interests of all bargaining unit members." The reasons given for this opposition center on the IAM's view that the Deming approach to management does not involve "a real sharing of power between unions and management."[38]

In fact, union-management committees set up to guide the implementation of TQM often do not give the union equal weight in decisions. What is more, the IAM sees the union's ability to veto any proposed action as crucial, but some union-management committees may not permit a union veto. Sometimes such committees have special powers to take actions outside or even in violation of certain terms of the union's contract. At least some union leaders see this as a dangerous precedent that threatens the legitimate authority of the union.

More subtly, union leaders may fear that successful TQM will reduce or remove the need for the union, since management voluntarily gives employees benefits (such as more meaningful jobs, greater autonomy, and increased authority) as well as sharing profits derived from productivity and performance gains and quality improvements. These outcomes would otherwise be obtainable only through union negotiation.

The IAM proposes to avoid this problem by restricting its approval to programs based on "the structural exclusion of management from a direct relationship with the rank and file." It is the IAM's position that this will ensure that the union will not be "bypassed" by management.[39] Other unions, too, have expressed misgivings about TQM. New Directions, a dissident splinter group within the United Auto Workers (UAW) union, also opposes union-management cooperation, which they call "jointness." They believe that the auto makers have taken advantage of union "givebacks" and cooperative efforts by eliminating jobs and reducing union power.

As described in a recent book by Joseph and Suzy Fucini, New Directions got its start at Mazda's Flat Rock, Michigan, plant.[40] Mazda agreed not to oppose, indeed to support, unionization in exchange for certain concessions from the UAW. One was to have just two job classifications, production worker and skilled trades, to increase flexibility. Another was the right to establish its own work rules without union "interference." The workers were carefully selected and trained in teamwork and consensus decision making. They were told that they would be involved in designing their work and even in purchasing equipment. So far this sounds like some of the success stories we told in Chapter Five. But reality intervened.

Soon after start-up both workers and managers began protesting—and quitting. American managers had expected to manage the plant. They found that they were only expected to carry out the orders of higher-level Japanese managers and executives. Employees had expected to design their own jobs, but they found they were compelled to follow the programmed worksheets provided by Mazda engineers, worksheets that spelled out every step of every job. There were no purchasing decisions to be made. All the tools and equipment had already been bought and set up.

In sum, workers found that the plant was closer to an old-fashioned time and motion study–designed system, albeit with self-regulating teams instead of constant and intensive supervision and monitoring. Many employees quit; turnover was much higher than anticipated. And when they had the chance, the workers voted out their union reps, despite interference by both the company and the UAW. And so New Directions was born. However, the sources of the greatest problems, the work pace and the high injury rate, were not subject to negotiation due to the original contract agreed to by the UAW.

It should be clear that the conditions at Mazda's Flat Rock plant as laid out by Fucini and Fucini bear no resemblance to TQM. In fact, the plant design seems to operate on the basis of Frederick Taylor's "scientific management," complete with time and motion study, not on Deming's fourteen points.

There is no doubt that other abuses of the sort just outlined have occurred, sometimes in subtle ways and sometimes almost openly. Recall how some firms saw in quality control circles an opportunity to squeeze a little more out of employees. And in bad times they did not hesitate to lay off many of those who had tried to help improve the organization's products and services. Similarly, some organizations have tried to use TQM and related approaches to reduce union power. This aim often includes increasing management control over workers and getting more out of employees while reducing costs.

Some believe that this is the only underlying purpose of TQM and team concepts. In their book, *Choosing Sides*, Mike Parker and Jane Slaughter argue that the intent of TQM is to "stress the system" so as to identify weak links, such as a few seconds of "wasted" time, and then "correct" them. This forces workers to perform at their maximum level of effort until they literally burn out.[41] We do not agree that this is part of any sound TQM approach. While the sort of abuses detailed by Parker and Slaughter and by Fucini and Fucini have no doubt occurred, we see them as perversions of TQM, not as typical examples. Such efforts are certain to fail. People quickly discover such hidden agendas and find creative ways to subvert them. Moreover, it is important to keep in mind that these are *not* examples of TQM.

There are two basic ways to guarantee that the sorts of threats perceived by union leaders that we defined earlier do not appear. One is to give the union full partnership as equals with management on any labor-management committee. Such a partnership would include the power to veto any proposed action. The second is to share equitably with employees gains in profit due to TQM-based improvements in quality, performance, and productivity. There must be rewards for these results and this must be a part of the organization's culture. Plans that increase employees' ownership stake based on profitability gains can help.

Trying to get around the union, reduce its power, and perhaps even eliminate it are actions inconsistent with TQM. Such actions make it impossible to create a climate of trust and may actively promote a climate of fear. Without trust, people cannot believe that the principle of equity holds. Fairness will not be an element of the organization's culture. Eventually all the TQM culture elements will be undermined. It is, then, especially important that unions be directly and formally involved in any TQM plans, as full and equal partners.

### But What Does the Union Get?

Until now we have been discussing union reactions to perceived threats from management, threats that seem to involve TQM. Still, even if management follows our advice and seeks to develop a real partnership with the union, one might ask what benefit there is for the union. Why should unions respond positively and engage in such TQM partnerships with management? It is one thing to not be attacked but quite another to identify a positive reason for unions to become involved in TQM.

Our answer is not original, but we believe it to be sound. There is ample evidence that unions must find and fulfill new missions if they are to survive, let alone prosper, in the next century.[42] One way for this to happen is by creating union-management partnerships that develop and support the high level of involvement and cooperation needed for TQM to succeed. Such real partnerships are possible. Both Germany and Japan, two of America's chief economic competitors, have higher levels of unionization than the United States.[43] And while union membership has decreased by almost half in the United States over the past twenty years, it has not changed in Japan or Germany. John Hoerr describes in the *Harvard Business Review* how German unions *contribute* to competitiveness rather than standing in the way.[44]

Of course, unionism is somewhat different both in Japan and in Germany. In Japan in the 1950s, the major automakers succeeded in breaking the once-powerful auto unions. The result is that in Japan all unions are company, not national, unions. To survive and thrive, which they have done, the unions have had to pursue a course of cooperation, not confrontation, with management.[45] In Germany, unions have much greater legal involvement in their organizations, typically having the right to sit on corporate boards. This gives the union a share of real responsibility for organizational performance, since the union has a voice in major top-level decisions. The way union-management relations are legally structured in Germany thus appears to encourage cooperation. In very different ways, union and management in Japan and Germany have developed patterns of cooperation that seem to have had substantial benefits both for labor and management.

Applying such lessons to American industry means that unions must move beyond representation to real involvement. Union leaders, as well as top management executives, will need vision. For example, in the United States joint union-management committees often have special authority to act in ways that would otherwise violate the contract. We have already noted the IAM's objection to such special arrangements. One alternative to special exceptions is to rewrite the contract itself.

This is precisely what union and management did at Shell Canada's Sarnia, Ontario, chemical plant. Management and the Energy and Chemical Workers Union, working together, prepared a new contract to serve as the basis for a vision of joint union-management responsibility. Then they designed a new plant structure. Teams of workers now run the plant, without supervisors. John Hoerr observes, "There is little rule making at Sarnia; instead, labor and management make decisions based on values expressed in a philosophical statement."[46]

Can it happen here? It has. Tom Peters describes how, in the early 1980s, the UAW and Cadillac worked together in Cadillac's Livonia, Michigan, engine plant.[47] Managers, union leaders, and hourly employees were members of a planning team that worked full time for about a year. Together, they came up with plans for the plant's organization and operation. They developed the

Livonia Engine Plant Operating Philosophy. The approach they took emphasizes partnership between labor and management. It also incorporates the team approach used at Shell Sarnia. One result of the efforts at Cadillac is clear: In 1990 Cadillac won the Malcolm Baldrige National Quality Award.

In various ways unions can help keep management honest. Some people, for example, argue that rewards for results, secure jobs, and equitable payment are not crucial elements of TQM. We believe they are. TQM based solely on recognition and other symbolic rewards may seem to be effective, for a while. However, we do not believe that such systems can be sustained over time. Because they have negotiating power, unions can ensure that there are rewards for results and that jobs remain at least as secure as they were before TQM. Unions may even help spur employee ownership. And they can buck the tendency to assume that recognition and symbols are TQM.

Unions can support new work designs, like the setup at Shell Sarnia just mentioned. Another way that unions can play a positive and important role is by encouraging employee ownership. The United Steelworkers Union is now involved in ESOPs in 25 companies. And unions can work with management to take a more active role in employee training. The UAW now runs training institutes in partnership with the auto makers, as does the Communications Workers of America with AT&T.[48]

In the fall of 1991 UAW members working at GM's new Saturn plant in Spring Hill, Tennessee, staged a demonstration, coming to work wearing black arm bands. But their aim was not to secure an increase in wages or benefits. What they sought was a delay in switching from a guaranteed base wage to a pay plan with a 20% productivity incentive. Why wouldn't they want the chance to earn more? Because various manufacturing problems had not been fully resolved. These union employees felt that quality could not be assured if productivity was sped up before the problems were dealt with. The workers wouldn't lose money—they might even earn more. But quality would suffer. That's why they demonstrated. Management eventually agreed with them. The president of Saturn admitted the union was right, and the new pay plan was delayed.

With a degree of vision on the part of leadership, unions can be the force that tilts the organizational balance toward TQM. Hoerr and others have observed that because the union can say "no," its choice in saying "yes" can be an important, perhaps essential, factor in driving TQM success.[49] As corporations change, unions, too, must change. This is the essence of a joint partnership approach to TQM.

## Cultural Leadership: Conclusions

Many of the examples and cases we cited earlier involved production or manufacturing organizations. In discussing how leaders build cultures, however, we have purposely tried to give examples from service, sales, and school organizations, all outside the traditional manufacturing arena. TQM and the cultural leadership needed to develop it are applied in much the same way in all types of organizations, not just in factories. The tools one uses may appear a bit different in a school, a service organization, or a factory. Still, the TQM values and, for the most part, the cultural elements that support TQM will be the same. And in every case it is culture-building leadership that creates TQM.

Unions have a role to play, too. This role involves much more than simply not acting to obstruct TQM. Union leaders who can participate in defining and constructing a vision, based on a partnership with management, can help create TQM cultures. The need for culture-building leadership is great. Such leadership must come from both union and management.

This leadership commitment means that CEOs and top executives must devote considerable personal time and effort as well as organizational resources to the TQM effort. Some quality consultants claim that quality is free, but it is not. TQM calls for a lot of hard work, along with capital investment. Organizations must commit a variety of resources if they are to implement the changes that we have described. Top-level leaders will probably find themselves spending half their time or more on TQM concerns.

When put into practice as TQM, through top-level leadership using the strategies described here, the programs, policies, and actions we have described will produce a TQM culture. And the results have been demonstrated, repeatedly, to be very positive in terms of long-term organizational effectiveness, that is, in terms of profit, performance, and quality.

Throughout our discussion of leadership we used examples involving Max De Pree and his company, Herman Miller. The firm is unusual in many ways. For example, De Pree denies that his organization is market driven. It is, he asserts, "a research-driven product company." Instead of simply finding out what customers want and producing products that satisfy them, Herman Miller aims "to meet the unmet needs of our users with problem-solving design and development."[50] The firm pioneered in quality design and manufacture. The Eames chair, named for its designer Charles Eames, is a good example. Samples are in the permanent collection of the New York Museum of Modern Art and the Louvre in Paris as examples of classic design. Most if not all the TQM culture-building factors described here have been in place at Herman Miller for generations. The Scanlon Plan for gainsharing has been used since 1952, and participative management and employee stock ownership have been in place almost as long.

What makes Max De Pree and Herman Miller a special example, however, is the bottom line. The firm is considered one of the hundred best places to work in America. In 1988 a *Fortune* magazine poll rated it fourth among *all* American companies in quality of products and one of the ten most-admired U.S. firms. Over the decade from 1975 to 1985, Herman Miller stock had a compound annual growth rate of 41%. The company recently ranked 456th in total sales among the Fortune 500, but it was ranked *7th* of the 500 in total return on investment over ten years. The bottom line shows that quality can pay very well indeed.[51]

Recently we asked a publisher of newsletters and books aimed at managers about his interest in a book proposal. He was pleasant but negative. He explained that his sales of consumer-focused materials were far greater than sales of materials aimed at helping managers improve their organizations. He said, "I'm not sure that managers really want to run their businesses well—too [much] hard work." In the next chapter we will look at some evidence to help judge whether our publisher friend was right to be so gloomy. We will also offer some first-step action suggestions for those not afraid of hard work.

## Endnotes

1. The pioneer of job enrichment is Frederick Herzberg. For details see his classic article "One More Time: How Do You Motivate Employees?" (*Harvard Business Review*, January/February 1968, pp. 53–62). This is one of the most requested and most reprinted articles that *Harvard Business Review* has ever published.

2. For more details, see Kenneth W. Thomas and Betty A. Velthouse, "Cognitive Elements of Empowerment," *Academy of Management Review*, October 1990, pp. 666–681.

3. William J. Paul, Jr., Keith B. Robertson, and Frederick Herzberg, "Job Enrichment Pays Off," *Harvard Business Review*, March/April 1969, pp. 61–78.

4. Donald N. Michael, "A Cross-Cultural Investigation of Closure," *Journal of Abnormal and Social Psychology*, 1953, pp. 225–230.

5. M. D. Kilbridge, "Reduced Costs Through Job Enrichment: A Case," *Journal of Business*, 1960, *33*, pp. 357–362.

6. Frederick Herzberg in the work cited in note 1.

7. Marshall Sashkin, *Making Participative Management Work* (King of Prussia, PA: Organization Design and Development, 1988).

8. Richard E. Walton, "How to Counter Alienation in the Plant," *Harvard Business Review*, November/December 1972, pp. 70–81. For a reconsideration of this case, see Walton's article "From Control to Commitment in the Workplace," *Harvard Business Review*, March/April 1985, pp. 76–84.

9. Rollin Glaser, *Moving Your Team Toward Self-Management* (King of Prussia, PA: Organization Design and Development, 1990).

   Rollin Glaser (Ed.), *Classic Readings in Self-Managing Teamwork* (King of Prussia, PA: Organization Design and Development, 1992).

10. Richard E. Walton, "From Control to Commitment in the Workplace," *Harvard Business Review*, March/April 1985, pp. 77–94.

11.  Aaron Bernstein and Associates, "Global Economy" (cover story). *Business Week*, August 10, 1992, pp. 49–53.

12.  See Chapter Eleven, "Job Design," in Marshall Sashkin and William C. Morris, *Organizational Behavior: Concepts and Experiences* (Englewood Cliffs, NJ: Reston Publishing Company/a Prentice-Hall company, 1984).

13.  Chris Argyris makes this point in detail in his classic book *Personality and Organization* (New York: Harper & Row, 1957).

14.  David C. McClelland has researched this basic human motive for many years. A good summary of his results can be found in his book *The Achieving Society* (New York: Irvington, 1976). In an earlier book, he shows how the achievement motive can be developed and supported organizationally. See David C. McClelland and David G. Winter, *Motivating Economic Achievement* (New York: Free Press, 1969).

15.  The human need for task-related (not simply social) interaction at work is best expressed in the research and writings of those involved with the sociotechnical systems approach to the study of organizations. See William A. Pasmore and John J. Sherwood, *Sociotechnical Systems: A Sourcebook* (San Diego, CA: University Associates, 1978).

16.  Marshall Sashkin, *Making Participative Management Work* (King of Prussia, PA: Organization Design and Development, 1988).

17.  Corey Rosen, Katherine J. Kline, and Karen M. Young, *Employee Ownership in America: The Equity Solution* (Lexington, MA: Lexington Books, 1986).

18.  Richard J. Long, "Job Attitudes and Organizational Performance Under Employee Ownership," *Academy of Management Journal*, December 1980, pp. 726–737.

19.  Douglas M. Cowherd and David I. Levine, "Product Quality and Pay Equity between Lower-level Employees and Top Management: An Investigation of Distributive Justice Theory." *Administration Times Quarterly*, June 1, 1992, 37, pp. 302–320.

20. Mitchell Fein, "Job Enrichment: A Reevaluation," *Sloan Management Review*, Winter 1974, pp. 69–88.

21. Rafael Aguayo, *Dr. Deming, the American Who Taught the Japanese About Quality* (New York: Carol Publishing Group, 1990).

22. Marshall Sashkin and Richard L. Williams have developed a variety of assessment and training materials to help managers determine the climate of fairness in their organizations and then improve it. See Marshall Sashkin, *The Managerial Mirror*, and Richard L. Williams *The Managerial Mirror Participant Workbook*, both published in 1990 by Organization Design and Development, Inc. (King of Prussia, PA). See also Marshall Sashkin and Richard L. Williams, "Does Fairness Make a Difference?" *Organizational Dynamics*, Autumn 1990, pp. 56–71.

23. William T. Morris points out, "Approaches to increased productivity are destined to be only fads if they are restricted to simple formulations such as job enrichment, participative management, or organizational development." See William T. Morris, *Work and Your Future: Living Poorer, Working Harder* (Reston, VA: Reston Publishing Co., 1975, p. 117).

24. Richard J. Long says, "The extent to which [employee ownership] is able to bring about increased [participative decision making] may be the single greatest factor affecting the success of employee ownership." See the work cited in note 17.

25. Terrence E. Deal and Alan Kennedy, *Corporate Cultures* (Reading, MA: Addison-Wesley, 1982.

26. For examples of how consultants have flocked to work in the field of organizational culture, see Bro Uttal's report "The Corporate Culture Vultures," *Fortune*, October 17, 1983, pp. 66–72.

27. Edgar H. Schein, "Organizational Culture," *American Psychologist*, February 1990, pp. 109–119.

28. Terrence E. Deal and Kent D. Peterson, *The Principal's Role in Shaping School Culture* (Washington, DC: GPO, 1990).

   Marshall Sashkin and Molly G. Sashkin, "Leadership and Culture Building in School: Quantitative and Qualitative Understandings."

Paper presented at the annual meeting of the American Educational Research Association, Boston, April 20, 1990 (ERIC Document ED 322 583).

29.    Brian Dumaine, "Creating a New Company Culture," *Fortune*, January 15, 1990.

30.    Joseph R. Jablonsky, Implementing Total Quality Management (Albuquerque, NM: *Technical Management Consortium*, 1990).

31.    Max De Pree, *Leadership Is an Art* (New York: Doubleday, 1989, p. 9).

32.    See the work cited in note 29.

33.    Benjamin B. Tregoe, John W. Zimmerman, Ronald A. Smith, and Peter M. Tobia, *Vision in Action: Putting a Winning Strategy to Work* (New York: Simon & Schuster, 1989), pp. 37–38.

34.    Mark A. Frohman and Marshall Sashkin, "Achieving Organizational Excellence: Development and Implementation of a Top Management Mind Set." Paper presented as part of a symposium, "Achieving Excellence," at the annual meeting of the Academy of Management, San Diego, August 1985.

35.    See the work cited in note 29, pp. 103–104.

36.    Peter M. Senge, *The Fifth Discipline* (New York: Doubleday/Currency, 1990).

37.    Peter M. Senge, "The Leader's New Work: Building Learning Organizations," *Sloan Management Review*, Fall 1990, pp. 7–23.

38.    These and further details are reported in an article by Frank Swoboda, "Union Leader: Managers Pull the Strings in 'Team' Programs," *Washington Post*, April 14, 1991.

39.    For additional details, see the work cited in note 36.

40.    Our summary of this case is based on the report by Joseph J. Fucini and Suzy Fucini in their book *Working for the Japanese: Inside Mazda's American Auto Plant* (New York: Free Press, 1990).

41.    Mike Parker and Jane Slaughter, *Choosing Sides: Unions and the Team Concept* (Boston: South End Press, 1988).

42.    For an excellent overview and current discussion, see the article by John Hoerr, "What Should Unions Do?" *Harvard Business Review*, May/June 1991, pp. 30–45. Many of the ideas in the discussion that follows are based on specific concepts and concerns identified by Hoerr.

43.    See the work cited in note 40, p. 30.

44.    See the work cited in note 40, pp. 37–39.

45.    We are grateful to Jon Bird for this observation, based on his extensive personal experience in Japan.

46.    See the work cited in note 40, p. 42.

47.    Tom Peters, *Thriving on Chaos* (New York: Knopf, 1987), pp. 297–298.

48.    See the work cited in note 40, p. 42.

49.    This point is made in an article by economists Adrienne E. Eaton and Paula B. Voos in *Unions and Economic Competitiveness*, edited by Lawrence Mishel and Paula B. Voos (New York: M. E. Sharpe, 1991) cited on p. 39 of the work described in note 40.

50.    See the work cited in note 29, pp. 72–73.

51.    This information is taken from James O'Toole's foreword to Max De Pree's book *Leadership Is an Art*, cited in note 29.

# 7

# First Steps Toward TQM

Our aim in writing this book was to help those who had heard of TQM figure out what the noise was all about. Is TQM just another management fad, or are there some useful ideas there for managers and organizations? While some aspects of TQM, such as quality circles, have assumed the dimensions of a fad, TQM itself is no fad. TQM has a fifty-year history of success in the United States and Japan.

Another purpose was to help readers make the right decision when deciding whether to pursue TQM for their organizations. Of course, we stated our bias openly to begin with. Many more American organizations must embrace TQM, not as a quick-fix fad but as a serious long-term endeavor. Unless they do, America's future as an international economic competitor is dim at best.

We have spoken often of Japan and Japanese successes with TQM. We have also tried to make it clear, from the beginning, that TQM is an American, not a Japanese, creation. The basic tools were developed by Americans: Shewhart, Deming, Juran, and others. The basic models of a management process and philosophy centered on quality for the customer were developed by Americans: Juran, Deming, and Feigenbaum, among others. And our basic understanding of organizational culture—how it's created and how it works—was developed by American scholars and practitioners: Parsons, Schein, Walton, and others.

Some elements of TQM culture, like employee ownership, are probably more common in America than in Japan. And we saw that at least one supposed application of TQM by a Japanese firm in the United States was probably not TQM at all. In sum, applying TQM does not mean accepting or adopting elements of Japanese culture, as some who criticize TQM have argued. Of course, neither is it a simple or easy matter.

We hope we have convinced you that difficult as TQM may be, it is less difficult and more desirable than economic failure. But we selected our examples not merely to show that TQM works and has business value. TQM has human value, too. Organizations with TQM cultures are not just more productive and effective, they are far better places for people to work. This is because TQM makes individual—as well as organizational—success more likely while encouraging conditions that meet human needs at work. TQM is not the lesser of evils. It has great positive value, both for organizations and for the people who make them work.

In this final chapter we have two aims. First we will, as promised in the introduction, define some first-step actions for those who wish to pursue TQM seriously. Then we will look to the future and the prospects it may hold for TQM.

## What First?

Different consultants have developed a wide range of TQM programs. Some programs are relatively straightforward, with a set of numbered steps and instructions. Others are complex, with manuals, charts, and software. Either kind of program can work effectively, depending on whether top executives are willing to take the lead in constructing a TQM culture.

We suggest three first steps, but we don't claim that any of them will be simple or easy. Nor will we guarantee that if you follow our advice you will succeed in creating a TQM culture. All we can promise is that if you carry out the following steps you will be ready to begin building a TQM culture—and we think you will have a good chance of success.

But before jumping into such a project, we suggest that you spend some time thinking about your organization's culture on your own. Consider whether the values and beliefs that make up the existing culture are in serious conflict with those needed to support TQM. If they are, think twice before starting something that might finish you before you finish it. One reason it's so hard to change organizational cultures is that they tend to be strong and stable and to resist such change efforts. Remember Sam, the plant manager; the culture that he had created lived on long after he died. If TQM values conflict with the values that you see in your organization, then you might be better off looking for some other route to organizational improvement.

### Step One: Top-Level Leadership Involvement and Direction

Paradoxically, TQM is led from the top, bottom up. That is, TQM works by empowering everyone, especially those at lower levels, and providing them with the knowledge and skills they need to take action commensurate with their work responsibilities. The purpose of such action is to improve quality for the customer. But equally important is leadership from the top to define and construct a TQM culture. Without cultural support, TQM becomes just another program, almost certain to fail eventually. And *only* leaders can construct such cultures. Thus, the first steps toward TQM require active, perhaps even vehement, support from the CEO.

If the CEO is not already committed, then the first step must be to develop understanding and active support at the top of the organization. Only then can the following steps succeed. In concept this is simple enough. Just educate the CEO and top executives about the content of this book. If that sounds easy, think again. Top executives aren't usually looking for ways to spend their leisure hours. And simple attention is not enough. You must also understand the content of this book well enough to convince the CEO that TQM is worth careful study.

While getting the attention and interest of top-level leaders is not easy, it is not impossible either. One way is to build many fires. That is, get lots of other people interested. Start a study group yourself. Begin to build a TQM culture in your own area and apply TQM to the extent that you can.

### Step Two: Create a Blue-Ribbon Study Group

Once top leadership makes a real commitment to TQM, the next step is to examine the organization and its culture. The CEO and top executives should be directly involved in a study group led by top management. This group examines the organization and assesses its current fit with and potential for TQM. This should be a careful and serious process of study, not just meetings to jaw about the basic ideas. The group should measure the organization with both quantitative tools (such as surveys) and qualitative evidence (cultural "artifacts" like traditions and stories). The group should include people from different parts of the organization and from different hierarchical levels, not just top managers. If there is a union, union leaders must be full members of the study group.

This group is much more likely to succeed if it has assistance from an expert outside consultant. The culture of an organization often works to hide important values and beliefs. Sometimes people just don't feel they can talk about these things. An outsider can help people uncover and come to grips with such facts. Even when there are no hidden secrets, we are still subject to blind spots. These are facts of organizational life that we have experienced for so long they seem like a natural part of the organization instead of our inventions. To make an analogy, it is hard for the fish to analyze the water it swims in, the onlyenvironment it knows. It is even harder for that fish to understand the nature of air.[1]

The aim of the study group is not just to increase awareness of TQM. The study group should have three to six months to carry out its assignment: a comprehensive study of the organization with a focus on its culture and the fit between that culture and TQM. The group's final report will determine whether and how TQM should be implemented. The conclusions of the study group should be formalized in a public final report. If the group concludes that the organization should pursue TQM, then the study group might also provide recommendations about specific next-step actions.

### Step Three: Establish an Action Task Force

If the study group report is positive, a long-term task force should be empaneled. Such a task force is often called a "quality council" or has some other TQM-relevant title. While the CEO and some top managers must be involved, others at various hierarchical levels and from various organizational units may also participate. This task force is empowered to develop a TQM plan and begin carrying it out. Top management may have to define a value-based philosophy as a first step. If a clear philosophy exists, the task might be to tie it to organizational operations through policies, programs, and leadership action.

These first, vision-based activities are important. They will make clear the nature of the organization's new commitment to TQM. But many people in the organization are still likely to be skeptical of top management's commitment to TQM. "It's just another program," they will say. Others will feel threatened, especially middle managers who fear that they will lose their control and perhaps even their jobs. Only through strong and persistent action can top leaders convince those who doubt and reassure those who fear. Task force actions must directly involve the CEO. Only this will show that TQM is not just another program but a real redirection of organizational action. And only the CEO can both assure mid-level managers that they will not be discarded as powerless leftovers and insist that they support rather than resist or oppose the change.

The action task force can also identify the need for and sponsor specific TQM projects and activities. Their work in this respect is based in good part on the thorough analysis done by the study group. Specific actions will depend on what the study group finds, on conditions in the organization, and on the work of those enlisted by the action task force for specific projects. Thus, we cannot offer step-by-step action guidelines. In general, every action proposal should be examined for its consistency with a value-based organizational vision centered on TQM. This is when the real work of implementing TQM begins. Our best advice is, as Stephen Covey says, "Begin with the end in mind."[2]

## Implementing TQM

The approach that each organization takes to TQM will be, to a degree, unique. This is because every organization has its own culture, with certain special characteristics that imply specific needs. Moreover, organizations will differ in their applications of TQM simply because it must be the parties themselves who create the plans and actions. Many years ago open systems theorists coined the term "equifinality."[3] It means that there are many different routes to a particular destination. Or, to put it simply, there is more than one way to skin a cat! In the case of TQM, the "best" way depends on the preferences of those involved.

Involvement is crucial for success. No outside expert can "install" TQM. Our advice is to run, not walk, away from any expert who wants to sell you the "five basic phases" of TQM, the "sequence of seven secret steps," or some other snake oil. Beware in particular of two dangers. First, there are those who would set up a team structure that parallels but does not involve the actual work process of the organization. TQM must be part of the doing of work, not simply an add-on. Second, watch out for those who suggest that it is all done through a "quality assurance board" or some such high-level group that designs, directs, and implements the entire TQM process. TQM not only requires that everyone be involved, it mandates that everyone be empowered.

Still, we have seen, studied, and participated in enough TQM efforts to know that there are some components that are reasonably generic. There are three in particular. First, it will hardly be news when we again say that *top-level managers must initiate the TQM activity*. Only top leadership can develop a TQM culture. That's why we counseled top-level involvement and direction as a first step toward TQM. That first step should, we advised, be supported by a top-level study group led by the CEO and aided by a consultant. And it must be followed by establishing an action task force. This group, which includes the CEO and top managers, acts as a TQM policy and oversight group to initiate and coordinate TQM activities throughout the organization. But while TQM is led from the top, it works bottom up. Two remaining common components of TQM efforts help resolve this apparent paradox.

The second component involves one or more *cross-function teams.* These teams are composed of managers and employees from different levels and different parts of the organization. They tackle important work process and culture-related problems identified by the study group and targeted by the action task force. For example, the study group analysis will almost certainly uncover some cases in which poor coordination of work activities leads to quality and performance problems, simply because the sequence of activities has not been designed well. Reporting to the action task force or some similar group, a cross-function team can dig in and, along with those involved in these work activities, develop some recommendations for major redesign. At least some of those appointed to the team should have positions in the organizational areas being examined. Actions will depend on the approval of team plans and recommendations by top management and on the support of those directly involved in the work flow problems.

Cross-function teams can also study and redesign or develop new policies and programs to change, improve, or create certain culture elements. This may mean redesigning hiring policies to look for people with values that fit a TQM culture. Or it may mean creating a new long-term management development program and promotion policies to ensure that the organization's future leaders will be able to help maintain TQM. There might be more than one cross-function team, depending on the size and complexity of the organization. The TQM work of cross-function teams should follow the Pareto principle and focus on the most important 20% of all quality problems.

Cross-function teams can be very helpful in starting a TQM effort. First, they get people throughout the organization actively engaged in TQM activities. And they get employees' attention, showing that top management is serious about TQM. But whatever they accomplish, cross-function teams are not the central feature of TQM. If TQM is no more than a series of team efforts like this, then it is sure to fail. After a year or so, people will get tired. They will start to ask why their own work is not really different. And they will begin to resent the time the cross-function teams take from their "real" work. After two years, the TQM effort will quietly die out as people withdraw their effort and energy and as the cross-function team projects become less and less significant. Cross-function teams can provide a valuable jump start to TQM, but you can't run a car indefinitely on a jump start. Similarly, TQM cannot work or succeed solely on the basis of continuing cross-function team projects.

For long-term success, TQM efforts depend on a third common component: *empowered workers and work teams*. This is where the real work of TQM happens: identifying and solving problems and improving work processes. This work often requires modifying or redesigning jobs to be done by teams. Training may be needed to enable employees and teams to use their authority effectively. But massive TQM training efforts are rarely needed. Such training is almost never an appropriate first step toward TQM.

### Is This Training Really Necessary?

Organizations often overspend for training, providing extensive workshops that cover more statistical tools and techniques than employees ever need or can use. This is especially true when the organization mistakenly confuses tools and techniques with TQM, but it can happen even when TQM efforts are correctly focused. Effective training meets the needs of the customers: the trainees. It is designed to address the specific needs of participants. And such training often takes place in the work context, not in an off-site classroom.

For example, team members may need to learn to work together more effectively. An appropriate training approach would have a training consultant meet with the team to examine and deal with specific problems. If individuals need to learn to use certain TQM tools for collecting data and analyzing problems, they can best do so through guided practice involving their actual work. Effective TQM training is not "pantyhose training" where one size fits all.

In any case, the need for TQM training is often less extensive than managers and executives think. Most employees can learn the basic TQM tools quickly. And awareness and commitment are less the product of a training seminar than the result of action by the CEO and top managers.

Empowering employees requires action on the part of the CEO and top managers, who work in concert with an action team, which may be called the *TQM policy group*, the *quality council*, or any of several other formal names. The organization's culture will almost certainly have to be modified in various ways in addition to the redesign of jobs. For example, organizational policies, programs, and practices must be revised or created to support rewards for results and other of the culture elements that empower employees.

A TQM culture permits and encourages everyone to take actions that not only solve quality problems but result in continuous improvement in the way work is done and in work outcomes. Most such activity occurs at lower levels of the organization. That's what we mean when we say that TQM works bottom up. Yet only leadership from the CEO and top executives can create a culture that instills and supports TQM actions on the part of lower-level employees. That's what we mean when we say TQM works from the top down. And that is our explanation for the paradox of total quality management, a system that depends on leadership and action from the top down *and* from the bottom up.

## What Does the Future Hold?

Will it happen? Will American organizations, in meaningful numbers, begin to move toward real (as opposed to sham or feigned) TQM? Will we see change in action or only in vocabulary and rhetoric? It is too soon to tell, but there are some positive indications. Awareness of the importance of quality and organizational interest in TQM are on the rise. Each year, more organizations apply for the Malcolm Baldrige National Quality Award.

Survey results show that Juran's and Walton's predictions of the trend toward self-managing teams are in fact accurate and in process. The most successful organizations, those in the Fortune 1000, are the ones moving most quickly in this direction.

Finally, consider a recent situation faced by top management of GM's new Saturn division and the action they took. Saturn is GM's new nameplate. Its aim is to challenge the Japanese by building an inexpensive small car of very high quality. Auto industry experts believe that in its first model year (1991) Saturn cars have been as good as any Japanese-built autos in their price range. Built in Spring Hill, Tennessee, in a new plant designed from the ground up, Saturn was given considerable autonomy from the GM bureaucracy. Both the latest technology and the principles of TQM culture are basic to the Saturn organization.

The event we refer to was widely reported in May 1991, when Saturn's management publicly announced both the problem and the action taken by the company. They discovered that more than a thousand cars had been delivered with improperly mixed chemical antifreeze that could damage the cooling system. Each person who had purchased one of the vehicles received a personal call, with an invitation to return the car and select a new one.

Saturn also listens to the voice of the customer. Cars were to get airbags in the fall of 1993, but customers wanted airbags immediately. Saturn's chief engineer says, "We put together a small product development team and said 'You guys have to have it ready for 1992.'" The team was empowered to make decisions and take action. The airbags were available in the spring of 1992, ahead of schedule.⁴ The major remaining problem is producing enough cars to meet customer demand. Saturn buyers are, according to the standard industry surveys conducted by J. D. Powers, more satisfied than Mercedes customers as well as more loyal than Lexus or Infiniti buyers.⁵

However, there are also some discouraging signs. The desire for quality awards, such as the Deming Prize or the Baldrige Award, has become so great among top managers that incredible efforts have been directed toward winning awards instead of toward TQM and quality improvement. Florida Power and Light (FP&L) devoted years of very costly effort to winning a foreign-organization version of the Deming Prize. FP&L, however, is now in financial trouble, and its customer satisfaction record is considerably worse than that of other Florida utilities. The extreme efforts devoted to winning the Deming Prize had, suggested *Fortune* magazine, pushed FP&L close to the organizational version of a nervous breakdown.⁶ In the past two years the CEO and the vice-president for quality were removed because of their debilitating prize-oriented efforts.

In another case, the Wallace Company, a 1990 Baldrige Award winner, has filed for Chapter 11 bankruptcy protection. The CEO admits that the company's exuberant efforts first to win and then to promote its winning of the Baldrige may have contributed to its financial problems. One result of these situations is the perception among some managers—and the public—of TQM as just another faddish management program.

Sometimes the reaction to TQM "failures" such as those of FP&L and the Wallace Company, is to reject the entire concept. One management consulting firm insists that those involved in TQM are "like lemmings marching to the sea."[7] This firm and some others argue that we must return to a clear focus on quick short-term results. They claim to identify TQM flaws, but their claims are based on misunderstandings and half-truths. They say, for example, that TQM means starting "dozens of quality activities" all at the same time, making it impossible to identify cause and effect. This is "like researching a cure for a disease by giving a group of patients ten different new drugs at the same time." The comparison is, of course, meaningless. TQM efforts don't involve a search for magic-bullet cures. TQM calls for careful identification of problems followed by corrective actions, actions that change the system for the better. Nor is there any need to suddenly initiate dozens of activities, although after a year or two the number of TQM activities is likely to be large if the organization has moved effectively toward TQM.

Results, these same consultants say, can be achieved in a month or two at most by setting challenging goals and telling people to do what needs to be done to meet these goals. They are, in one sense, correct. People *will* meet the goals. But at what cost? Instead of taking the time to develop real solutions to problems, they will do whatever they must do to show results, often to the detriment of the organization. Deming gives an instructive example when he tells of an out-of-town manager who asked to meet with him early in the morning.[8] But this would require the manager to go to the airport at two in the morning. He asked why she didn't just come the night before. The manager said that her company would not pay for a hotel room. Their travel department also got a special discount on the early flight. The travel department, with a goal of cost savings, "gets a plus," says Deming, but the manager arrives "totally unfit to go to [the] meeting." The travel department should be working to get the manager "on the job fit for the job." But their short-term goal is to save money. "Can you blame them for doing it?" says Deming. "Saving money, ruining the company." This is an example of what nonsystemic short-term goals and results-oriented pressures can do. Yes, the travel department meets its goal and looks good, but at what long-term cost to the company?

The *Wall Street Journal* recently reported the results of a survey of 1237 corporate employees conducted by Gallup for the American Society for Quality Control.[9] Over 50% reported that their organizations say that quality is a top priority. But only one-third said that their companies followed through on such claims. And fewer than one-sixth felt their companies gave them real control over work decisions, a crucial aspect of TQM culture.

A later article in the *Wall Street Journal* suggested that "the quality movement . . . appears to be losing some of its allure." This conclusion was based on the lack of extensive application in several important industries. For example, only 19% of American banks responding to a survey used customer complaints to identify new products or services. The figure was higher for computer makers, 26%, but in Germany it was 60%, and in Japan it was 73%. One consultant put part of the blame on the isolation of quality programs from day-to-day operations, much as we discussed earlier in this chapter.[10]

It will not be easy for American firms to move all the way to the third, culture-change level of TQM. The first level, use of the tools, is easy, though often a dead end. The second level, an explicit and serious focus on quality for the customer, is more difficult to achieve. Companies often try this only when there is no other option to staunch profitability losses. But organizations must move even further. They must internalize the underlying values and beliefs needed to make TQM effective. Otherwise, the result will be abandonment of the effort and of TQM.

Only through leadership can organizations move to full, culture-based TQM. One well-known organizational psychologist has said it may be that the *only* really important thing leaders do is create organizational cultures.[11] But he also expressed doubt that leaders of American organizations can make the cultural changes that are needed. Warren Bennis, who has defined the culture-building strategies that leaders use, has also written eloquently of the barriers that potential visionary leaders face.[12]

Stephen Covey gives helpful guidance when he observes that to create a TQM culture leaders must begin from the inside out, that is, with personal (not simply personnel) changes. The development of character described by Covey is a process involving consider-able work.[13] He refers to principles involving trust, empowerment, and organizational alignment. These are, of course, aspects of the culture elements that we described in Chapter Five.

Despite the difficulties and obstacles faced by leaders who would shape organizational culture, we are optimistic about the potential for success. Both scholars and practitioners know much more about leadership and its dynamics today than just a few years ago, thanks to the work of such scholars as Bennis[14] and practitioners like Max De Pree.[15]

We are beginning to understand how leaders construct organi-zational cultures. There is nothing simple or easy about it, but there is hope that, through visionary leadership, organizations can be transformed by cultures founded on total quality management.

In sum, the future holds what leaders and followers choose to build into it. It is a matter of choice, and the choice is up to us. Some years ago, an interviewer asked W. Edwards Deming whether he required a certain number of years of commitment from an organization before he would agree to work with it on quality improvement. His answer: "Forever."[16]

## Endnotes

1. This concept was first stated by Marshall McLuhan in his classic text *Understanding Media* (New York: McGraw-Hill, 1964).

2. Stephen R. Covey, *The Seven Habits of Highly Effective People: Restoring the Character Ethic* (New York: Simon & Schuster, 1989), pp. 96–144.

3. See Chapter One in Daniel Katz and Robert L. Kahn, *The Social Psychology of Organizations* (New York: Wiley, 1966; rev. ed. 1978).

4. Warren Brown and Frank Swoboda, "Saturn's Design Turns on a Dime." *Washington Post,* July 6, 1992.

5. David Woodruff and Associates, "Saturn" (cover story) *Business Week,* August 17, 1992, pp. 79–91.

6. *Fortune,* July 1, 1991.

7. Ronald Ashkenas and Robert Schaffer, "The Lemmings Who Love Total Quality," *New York Times,* May 3, 1992, Business Section, p. 13.

8. Interview, *Wall Street Journal,* June 1, 1990.

9. Amanda Bennett, "Quality Programs May Be Shoddy Stuff," *Wall Street Journal,* October 10, 1990, p. 81.

10. Gilbert Fuchsberg, "Quality Programs Show Shoddy Results," *Wall Street Journal,* May 14, 1992, pp. B1, B7.

11. Edgar H. Schein, *Organizational Culture and Leadership* (San Francisco: Jossey-Bass, 1985).

12. For a detailed description of how leaders act strategically to build culture, see Warren Bennis and Bert Nanus, *Leaders: The Strategies for Taking Charge* (New York: Harper & Row, 1985). On the problems that leaders face, see Warren Bennis, *Why Leaders Can't Lead: The Unconscious Conspiracy Continues* (San Francisco: Jossey-Bass, 1989).

13. See the work cited in note 2.

14. W. Bennis, *On Becoming a Leader* (Reading, MA: Addison-Wesley, 1989).

15. Max De Pree, *Leadership Is an Art* (New York: Doubleday, 1989).

16. Quoted in an interview by Dan Gottlieb in the *Washington Post,* January 15, 1984, p. D3.

# Appendix A

# The Seven Old Tools

The seven old tools are very basic, but very important. Deming's thirteenth point states that everyone must learn the basics of statistical theory and application, since this is the language of improvement. We have already referred to some of the seven tools; let us briefly define each one.

### Control Charts

Control charts display the results of statistical process control measures. Control charts tell several things. First, they show whether measures of a product or activity fit a normal, or bell-shaped, curve. (See our discussion in Chapter One for more detail.) If so, then the work process is "in control," because any variability in measures is random. Thus, variations are not due to some consistent outside error factor. Control charts provide a clear visual display that quickly tells one when a process is out of control. The production process can then be corrected and brought back into control.

In a normal distribution most of the measures are close to (though slightly different from) the overall mean or average; few things are ever *exactly* average. The typical or average difference of the random measures from the overall mean is called the *standard*

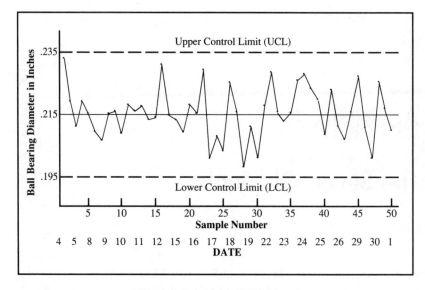

**Figure A: Control Chart**

*deviation* and is usually symbolized by the Greek letter *sigma* ($\sigma$). The standard deviation tells how variable a measurement is. If the measures form a normal distribution, then over 99% will fall somewhere between +3 and –3 standard deviations from the mean. That is, one would almost never find a case of a measure so high, so far above the mean, as to be more than three times the average difference from the mean. Nor would one expect to obtain a measure so low as to be below the mean by more than three times the average difference from the mean. So, +3 standard deviations is referred to as the *upper control limit* (UCL), while –3 standard deviations is called the *lower control limit* (LCL).

The UCL and LCL can be approximately calculated by knowing the average, the range, and the number of measures made. To set up a control chart one must obtain sample measures and then determine the average and the range. Then the UCL and LCL can be calculated, based on an estimate of variability and assuming a normal distribution. Every control chart shows the UCL and

LCL, so one can easily see whether the actual measures ever (or usually) exceed the UCL or go below the LCL.

Consider a ball bearing. One would take random samples of, say, the diameter of the ball bearings produced. The data would be used to calculate the UCL and LCL of a control chart. From then on a control chart could be used to track the production process. Samples would be taken at specific times, for example, every three hours. The data are plotted on the control chart, with the diameter on the vertical axis and time along the horizontal axis. All is well if the measurements all fall within the upper and lower control limits.

What if some ball bearings have a diameter greater than the UCL or smaller than the LCL? This means some ball bearings are so large or so small that they would not be there if the actual distribution of sizes forms a normal, bell-shaped curve. Thus, the distribution is not normal. And that, in turn, means that the process is not in control. When random sampling yields measurements above the upper control limit or below the lower control limit, this triggers a search for the cause of the problem; something is wrong and must be corrected.

Of course, even when the distribution of measures shows that the process is in control, the average may still be off-target, too high or too low. And the amount of variation may still be much greater than desired. A control chart can, however, also help identify the reasons for those conditions and can thus be important for changing them. Control charts are important and basic statistical process control tools.

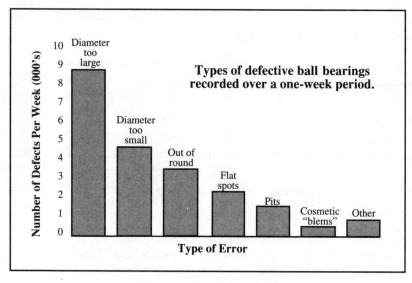

**Figure B: Pareto Chart**

## Pareto Charts

A Pareto chart is a simple tool, used to count and display the number of defects or problems of various types over a certain period of time. The results are displayed on a chart as bars of varying length. The underlying principle, based on the work of the nineteenth–century Italian economist Vilfredo Pareto, is that about 80% of all problems can be traced to only 20% of all the varied possible causes; the remaining 80% of causes account for only 20% of the problems and defects.[1]

To get the most out of improvement efforts one should always begin by attacking those few causes that are responsible for the majority of all quality problems. Pareto charts help identify the relatively few categories of causes that account for most problems. The chart can also be useful for identifying points in the production process at which defects of certain types are most likely to occur.

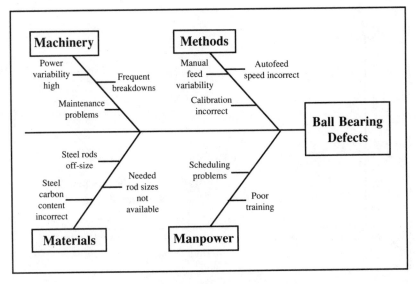

**Figure C: Fishbone Diagram**

### Fishbone Diagrams

These are also called *cause-and-effect diagrams* or *Ishikawa diagrams* (after Kaoru Ishikawa, who first developed this tool). The diagram looks somewhat like a fishbone, with the problem or defect—the *effect*—defined at the "head." On the "bones" growing out of the "spine" one lists possible causes of production problems, in order of possible occurrence. The chart can help point out how various separate problem causes might interact. It also shows how possible problem causes occur with respect to one another, over time, helping to start the problem-solving process.

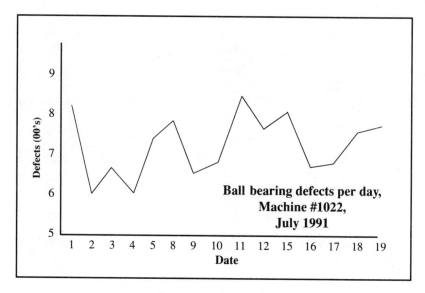

Ball bearing defects per day,
Machine #1022,
July 1991

**Figure D: Run Chart**

### Run Charts

Run charts, sometimes called *trend charts*, are used to display measurements made over specific time intervals—a day, a week, or a month, for example. One can then construct a graph, with the quantity measured on the vertical axis and time along the horizontal axis. A run chart is little more than a running tally. Its major use is to help determine whether there are critical times that problems of various types occur. One can then investigate why this is so. For example, a plot of defects by hour or day might show that problems consistently appear when materials from a certain supplier are used (as on July 11 in Figure D, above). This suggests that materials from that supplier might be the cause. Or, it may be found that a specific machine comes on line at the same time that certain problems appear, suggesting that the cause might lie with that machine.

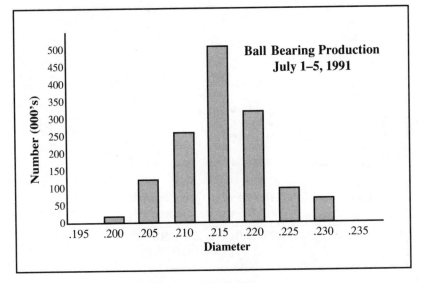

**Figure E: Histogram**

## Histograms

A histogram is also known as a *bar chart*. On this chart the number of products in each control category (that is, at each of a number of separate, measured values) is represented by the length of a bar. Each category is labeled and the bars are placed next to one another, horizontally or vertically. This shows which categories account for most of the measured values as well as the comparative size of each category. Histograms give a picture of the actual distribution of measures. They can show whether or not the distribution is normal (shaped roughly like a bell).

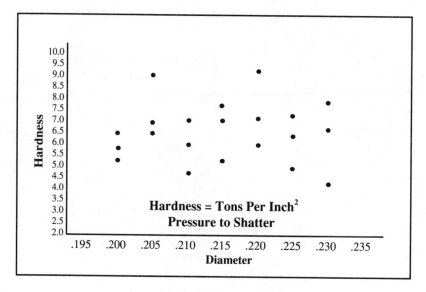

**Figure F: Scatter Diagram**

### Scatter Diagrams

Scatter diagrams provide a standard way of showing how one variable, for example, tensile strength of a wire, relates to another, such as the wire's diameter. In the example shown in Figure F, the strength of wire of various diameters was tested by pulling on the wire until it broke. The exact strength required to break each wire was then recorded. The results are graphed, with diameter on the horizontal axis and strength on the vertical axis. It is then possible to clearly see the relationship between wire tensile strength and wire diameter. This sort of information is useful for product design.

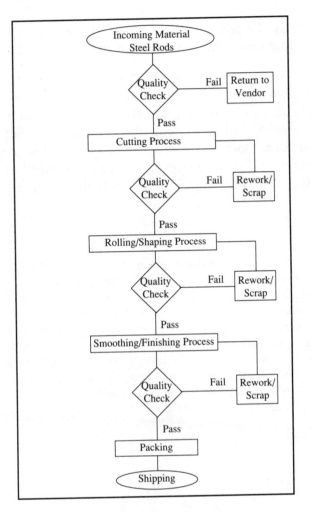

**Figure G: Flow Chart**

### Flow Charts

Flow charts, sometimes called *input-output charts*, give a visual description of the specific steps in a work activity. They can be extremely helpful for understanding exactly how things are being done and then determining how to improve that process. The procedure can be applied to the entire organization, too, to visually track and chart the way the organization operates.

Flow charts use certain standard symbols to refer to certain types of activities (such as decisions, shown by diamonds, and activities, shown by boxes) but these conventions are not as important as recording a clear description of the sequence of work activities. Flow charts can also be used to design improved work processes, by showing how things *should* happen and comparing this with the way things actually occur.

## Endnote

1.  Pareto studied the distribution of wealth in society. He demonstrated that a small proportion of the population accounted for (owned) a large proportion of all the wealth. The general principle—that most problems are the result of just a few causes, that most productive outcomes are due to just a few specific people, operations, or work units, and so on—was stated not by Pareto but by Joseph M. Juran, in the late 1940s. Having been inspired by Pareto's work, Juran named his general observation "the Pareto principle." Juran details all this in a brief article in the magazine *Quality Progress* (May 1975, pp. 8–9).

# Appendix B

# The Baldrige Award

The Malcolm Baldrige National Quality Award was established by a 1987 act of Congress. Up to two awards are made annually in each of three categories: manufacturing, service, and small business. The purpose is to recognize U.S. companies that excel in quality achievement and quality management. While modeled on the Deming Prize, requirements and procedures are not identical.

Applicants submit extensive, detailed documentation of their qualifications with respect to each of seven major examination categories. Each of the seven categories has two or more

---

*Note:* Most of the information contained in this appendix is quoted or adapted from the *1992 Application Guidelines: Malcolm Baldrige National Quality Award.* Single copies of the latest guidelines are available at no cost from:

> Malcolm Baldrige National Quality Award
> National Institute of Standards and Technology
> Gaithersburg, MD 20899
> Telephone: (301) 975-2036; Fax: (301) 948-3716

subcriteria or "items," with 28 specific items in all. Each category and each item in a category is assigned a certain point value, based on importance. Items are valued from 15 to 75 points, while the seven categories range from a low of 60 points to a high of 300.

Substantial fees are required of organizations that submit applications judged eligible to compete. For 1992, the charge is $4000 for manufacturing and service firms and $1200 for small business organizations. These fees cover only the costs of application reviews. There are additional charges for site visit reviews conducted for the relatively small number of applicants that successfully accomplish the following two stages of the review process.

In the first stage, applications are reviewed by a panel composed of four members of the 150-person board of examiners. The board members are quality experts selected from business, professional and trade organizations, accrediting bodies, universities, and government. Individuals apply for membership through a rigorous selection process. They then complete an examination preparation course that ensures a thorough understanding of the examination process, the specific items on the examination, how to use the scoring system, and how to prepare feedback reports.

There are three types of board members: examiners, senior examiners, and judges. The first review panel is composed of at least three examiners and one senior examiner, who leads the group. Their report is read by the panel of judges, which determines whether the application goes on to the second stage, called *consensus review.*

This second review is similar to the first, with a new group of at least three examiners and one senior examiner group leader. During this review, the panel of judges reviews the report to decide which applicants receive site visits.

The site visit review is conducted by at least five members of the board, led by a senior examiner. They visit the applicant's facilities and operating units, review records and data files, and interview corporate officials. They report their findings to the panel of judges.

The panel of judges reviews all of the site visit reports and makes recommendations on which applicants should receive awards. The National Institute of Standards and Technology receives these recommendations and presents them to the U.S. Secretary of Commerce, who makes the final decisions. After the awards have been announced, all applicants receive extensive feedback reports.

## Examination Categories and Items

The chart below shows the seven categories and the point value for each. The categories are broken down further into two to eight subcategories, or items, with each item having a specific point value (the 28 items are not shown on our chart).

| | Baldrige Award Criteria | Point Values |
|---|---|---|
| 1.0 | Leadership | 90 |
| 2.0 | Information and Analysis | 80 |
| 3.0 | Strategic Quality Planning | 60 |
| 4.0 | Human Resource Development and Management | 150 |
| 5.0 | Management of Process Quality | 140 |
| 6.0 | Quality and Operational Results | 180 |
| 7.0 | Customer Focus and Satisfaction | 300 |

The most important examination category is Customer Focus and Satisfaction. This supports one of the central points of this book, that is, the fact that the whole aim of TQM is quality for the customer. Customer Focus and Satisfaction is valued at 300 points, almost twice as much as any other examination category.

Three other examination categories are considered very important, valued at 140 points or more: Quality and Operational Results, Management of Process Quality, and Human Resource Development and Management.

The Quality and Operational Results category involves what we called *results metrics* in Chapter Five, but it does not refer just to inspection (Quality Checkpoint 2). Measures of the quality of results are taken at QC3, QC4, and QC5, as well as at QC2. These measures, however, are at the organizational level and do not reflect on individuals or identifiable work teams. This examination category is intended to provide comprehensive measures of the absolute level of quality obtained throughout the organization, in terms of results and outcomes.

Management of Process Quality refers to *process metrics* at QC2, QC3, QC4, and QC5. Each quality checkpoint is assessed by one or more of the specific items in this category. (Recall that QC1 is covered primarily by the customer satisfaction category.)

The Human Resource Development and Management category includes as items some of the eight TQM culture elements defined and discussed in Chapters Five and Six. For example, "employee performance and recognition" (rewards for results) is worth 25 points, while "employee involvement" (authority equal to responsibility) is worth 40 points. While a number of the items that make up each examination category relate to one or more of the eight TQM culture elements, the connections are generally indirect and implicit rather than clear and explicit, as in the two examples just cited.

In Chapter Six we discussed the importance of top-level leadership in constructing a TQM culture. The Leadership examination category is worth 90 points. Thus, the Baldrige Award does recognize that leadership has an explicit role to play in TQM, even though in our view the point value placed on leadership is a serious underestimation of its real importance.

The examination category Strategic Quality Planning also examines culture, asking whether there is a comprehensive organizational philosophy based on TQM. The category also includes items that assess whether this TQM philosophy is implemented through long-term planning, strategy development, and tactical implementation. The category as a whole is worth 90 points.

Information and Analysis, the examination category with the least total points—just 60—refers to the tools we described in Chapter Three. (Training for organization members in the use of the tools is assessed by an item included as part of the Human Resource Development and Management examination category.) The value assigned to Information and Analysis supports our view that tools, techniques, and training—while not unimportant—are actually the least crucial aspect of TQM.

## TQM and the Baldrige Award

Even the above brief review should make it clear that in concept the Baldrige Award is consistent with the view of TQM proposed in this book. What differences do exist are for the most part differences of emphasis, not substantial or substantive areas of conflict.

We feel obliged, however, to add a word of advice: Before deciding to pursue the Baldrige National Quality Award, top executives should reflect thoughtfully on their motives for doing so. The effort and the actual costs involved in competing for the Baldrige Award can be very great. While it may be tempting to "go for" the Baldrige to demonstrate to others the organization's quality orientation, this is actually a poor reason for applying. Firms that seek the Baldrige Award to gain publicity or to market the organization as a quality firm will find that such aims usually do not withstand the scrutiny that examiners give each applicant.

Perhaps the most dramatic negative example concerns not the Baldrige Award but the Deming Prize (actually, a special version of the Deming Prize set up recently for non-Japanese organizations). For several years, Florida Power & Light worked to prepare to compete. In 1990, FP&L won the Deming Prize for foreign (non-Japanese) organizations. But the efforts expended were so great, says Jeremy Main in *Fortune* magazine,[1] that the company came close to an organizational version of a nervous breakdown.

Main observed that FP&L now has a customer complaint record worse than several other Florida utilities. Earnings have decreased, costs have increased, and FP&L recently announced plans to lay off more than 2000 employees, an action completely out of character for an organization in which TQM is really in operation. (The vice-president for quality was also fired, and the CEO has been replaced.) One source of profit for the company, however, has been the unit that sells consulting services to other organizations interested in TQM. The central feature of their program is a step-by-step problem-solving/improvement process called the *QI* (quality improvement) *way*. But when the new CEO spoke with employees he reported widespread resentment. People told him that there was a preoccupation with process and with following the steps of the QI way. He said there seemed to be "less recognition for making good business decisions than for following the QI process."[2]

In hindsight, it is clear that FP&L went well beyond a reasonable level of effort, partly because the concern from the beginning was less with quality than with winning the prize. A real danger is the possibility that firms competing for the Baldrige may make the same mistake, forgetting or ignoring the real goal of quality improvement in favor of the short-lived publicity attained by winning the award.

Competing for quality prizes just to get publicity represents a terrible waste of resources and energy. In his *Fortune* article, Jeremy Main is understandably critical of firms that devote unreasonably great efforts to winning quality awards. But even a normal degree of effort is considerable. Most Baldrige Award winners spend several years working on TQM before even applying for the award (and we're talking *real* years here, not total staff time combined and presented as though one person were doing it all). Before winning the Baldrige Award, Globe Metallurgical, a relatively small organization, worked for four years to get ready to compete. It took Xerox five years to prepare. Motorola spent seven years.

Not only does the competition require a substantial up-front application fee and extensive staff time, winners are obligated to share what they have learned. In 1989, Motorola employees made 352 speeches to conventions and corporations, and Motorola responded to over a thousand inquiries from other companies. Senior executives of a small firm like Globe Metallurgical gave speeches in Singapore and Moscow, along with 134 less distant presentations.[3]

The Houston-based Wallace Company won a 1990 Baldrige. CEO John W. Wallace believes that the cost of the company's efforts to share its TQM learnings with others contributed to the firm's 1991 entry into Chapter 11 bankruptcy.[4] We suspect that misdirected energies, turned toward winning the Baldrige instead of applying TQM, also had something to do with the Wallace Company's problems.

With such cost and effort required, along with the real prospect of economic danger and the low probability of actually winning, why would any organization even want to compete for a Baldrige

Award? Winners and losers alike say that working for the Baldrige Award demonstrates in action their absolute commitment to TQM. And, in addition, they report that the most concrete reward is the feedback received.

David Kearns, former CEO of Xerox, says that 90% of the value of the process is in the feedback. David Luther, vice president for quality at Corning—a "loser"—says, "Its the cheapest consulting you can ever get."[5] The feedback received from its 1988 losing effort helped Milliken & Company to win the Baldrige in 1989. CEO Roger Milliken says, "Applying for the Baldrige and getting the feedback they give you is of incredible value to a company."[6] In sum, it is the feedback that makes the process worthwhile, feedback that tracks the organization's efforts and outcomes and helps to further advance the TQM process.

Some quality experts, including Deming, believe that competing for the Baldrige Award represents misdirected energy and effort. Indeed, opposition to the Baldrige Award is, according to Lloyd Dobbins, just about the only thing on which Deming and Philip Crosby agree.[7] David Snediker, vice-president for quality at Battelle, a behavioral science research center in Ohio, argues that firms should be competing for business, not for awards.[8]

Despite all this opposition and examples like those provided by FP&L and the Wallace Company, we must express qualified support for the Baldrige Award. That is, if efforts to achieve a Baldrige Award (or a Deming Prize) are part of an organization's active commitment to TQM, the payback can be well worth the cost. If, however, the intent is to win the award, whether to enhance the CEO's ego, to make a good impression with customers as a "quality oriented" company, or to simply enhance the organization's focus on results, then no expense and no amount of effort can be justified. Perhaps most distressing of all, the Baldrige guidelines and criteria have been revised to place even greater emphasis on bottom-line results as opposed to process control and improvement.[9]

## Endnotes

1.    Jeremy Main, "Is the Baldrige Overblown?" *Fortune*, July 1, 1991, pp. 62–65.

2.    See the work cited in note 1.

3.    Jeremy Main, "How to Win the Baldrige Award," *Fortune*, April 23, 1990, pp. 110–112, 116.

4.    Robert C. Hill and Sara M. Freedman, "Managing the Quality Process: Lessons from a Baldrige Award Winner," *The Academy of Management Executive*, February 1992, pp. 76–88.

5.    See the work cited in note 3, p. 112.

6.    See the work cited in note 3, p. 110.

7.    Lloyd Dobbins personal communication.

8.    See the work cited in note 3, p. 116.

9.    Gilbert Fuchsberg, "Baldrige Award Gives More Weight to Results." *Wall Street Journal*, February 24, 1992, p. B1.

# Appendix C

# Key Resources for TQM

This appendix provides some starting points to readers who are seriously interested in pursuing TQM. We will indicate which two or three books are absolute "must read" material, as well as where to go for help (with names and numbers). First, we list the major quality-related professional organizations and associations. Following that is our short list of major resources for each of the three basic aspects of TQM: tools, customer orientation, and culture.

## Organizations

American Society for Quality Control
310 West Wisconsin Avenue
Milwaukee, WI 53203
(414) 272-8575

American Quality and Productivity Center
123 N. Post Oak Lane
Houston, TX 77024
(713) 681-4020

Association for Quality and Participation
801-B West 8th Street
Cincinnati, OH 45203
(513) 381-1959

Quality and Productivity Management Association
300 N. Martingale Road, Suite 230
Schaumberg, IL 60173
(708) 619-2909

## Tools

### Books

The single best resource for publications about TQM tools is the Productivity Press, P.O. Box 3007, Cambridge, MA 02140 (Telephone: 617-497-5146). While their materials tend to be expensive, ranging from $40 for a book on total production maintenance to $3500 for a manual on how to implement a just-in-time manufacturing system, the materials are very current and cover just about every tool imaginable. A good place to start is the *Handbook of Quality Tools* by Kazuo Ozeki and Tetsuichi Asaka. Several of the other books published by Productivity Press appear in chapter endnotes throughout this book.

Another important publisher in this field is the Industrial Engineering and Management Press, a division of the Institute of Industrial Engineers (a major professional organization). IIE books concentrate more on management's role than on how to use specific quality control tools and techniques. For information and a list of current books, write to IIE, Publication Sales, 25 Technology Park, Norcross, GA 30092, or call (404) 449-0460.

One of the most widely used tool resources is a pocked-sized booklet *The Memory Jogger*, published by GOAL/QPC (Growth Opportunity Alliance of Greater Lawrence/Quality, Productivity, and Competitiveness). *The Memory Jogger* provides clear, brief, style instructions for using the seven old tools. GOAL/QPC has recently published unexpanded, full-sized book on tools—including some of the new tools—called *The Memory Jogger Plus* (by Michael Brassard). For more information, contact GOAL/QPC at 13 Branch Street, Methuen, MA 01844 (Telephone: 508-685-3900).

### Seminars/Technical Assistance

Productivity Press's parent organization, Productivity, Inc., conducts seminars and provides consultants on TQM. Their toll-free information number is (800) 888-6485 (Address: 101 Merritt 7 Corporate Park, Norwalk, CT 06851; Telephone: 203-846-3777). The Institute of Industrial Engineers also sponsors seminars and an annual national professional meeting that includes many workshops and seminars; see above for their address and telephone number.

Another high quality approach to learning and using tools and techniques is through seminars, conferences, and custom-designed training offered by GOAL/QPC. Contact GOAL/QPC at the address above.

## Quality for the Customer

### Books/Videos

There are any number of books on customer service, but most do not focus on TQM or quality in the sense used here. Some that do, or that approach such a focus are:

> William H. Davidow and Bro Uttal, *Total Customer Service* (New York: Harper & Row, 1989).

> Joseph M. Juran, *Juran on Quality by Design* (New York: Free Press, 1992).

> Joseph M. Juran, *Juran on Planning for Quality* (New York: Free Press, 1988).

Larry W. Kennedy, *Quality Management in the Nonprofit World* (San Francisco: Jossey-Bass, 1991).

Jay W. Spechler, *When America Does It Right: Case Studies in Service Quality* (Norcross, GA: Industrial Engineering Press, 1988).

A wide variety of additional relevant publications by Joseph M. Juran and his associates is available from the Juran Institute, Inc., 11 River Road, Wilton, CT 06897-0811 (Telephone: 203-834-1700; Fax: 203-834-9891).

For video materials we suggest examining some of the programs available from the Juran Institute. Two films produced by Britannica, Inc., "TQC/Manufacturing" and "TQC/Service," also give a sound basic introduction to TQM in terms of an integrated "quality for the customer" approach. Another fine video program, "Competing Through Quality," has been developed by David A. Garvin, Professor of Business Administration at Harvard, available from Nathan/Tyler, 535 Boylston Street, Boston, MA 02116.

### Seminars/Technical Assistance

The Juran Institute conducts many public seminars year-round in various major cities in the United States and abroad. These seminars focus on a systemic approach to managing for total quality, as mentioned in Chapter Four. For information, write or call the Juran Institute (see above).

## TQM Culture

### Books/Videos

Not an "easy read," but certainly the most TQM culture–focused book written by any of the recognized experts is Deming's classic *Out of the Crisis* (Cambridge, MA: MIT Center for Advanced Engineering Study, 1986). A more readable exposition of Deming's thought can be found in Mary Walton's book *The Deming*

*Management Method* (New York: Putnam Perigee, 1986). A more recent Deming-centered book, and one that may be more faithful to the views Deming expresses in *Out of the Crisis*, is Rafael Aguayo's *Dr. Deming: The American Who Taught the Japanese About Quality* (New York: Carol Publishing Group, 1990). A sense of the nature of TQM culture can be obtained by a careful reading of Tom Peters' *Thriving on Chaos* (New York: Knopf, 1988).

For a definitive view of TQM as a culture-change approach, see any or all of the sixteen volumes that comprise *The Deming Library*, available from Films, Inc. In particular we recommend Volume II, *The 14 Points*, and Volume X, *How Managers and Workers Can Change*.

### Seminars/Technical Assistance

W. Edwards Deming still conducts public seminars, some of which are offered through George Washington University in Washington, DC. You can write to Dr. Deming for information, at 4924 Butterworth Place, Washington, DC 20016.

The Center for Creative Leadership has developed a program, "Systems Leadership," focused on the strategies by which top executives use vision to build values relating to quality and excellence into their organizations' cultures. For information, contact the Center, P.O. Box 26300, 5000 Laurinda Drive, Greensboro, NC 27438-6300 (Telephone: 919-288-7210).

D. Scott Sink's seminar, "Being a Changemaster in Quality and Productivity Management," incorporates a strong focus on both quality for the customer and the nature of TQM culture. For information, contact the Virginia Productivity Center at Virginia Tech in Blacksburg (Telephone: 703-231-4568).

# Index

# Now Available . . .

## *Total Quality Management Assessment Inventory*

The *Total Quality Management Assessment Inventory* is designed to help an executive team understand the culture of the organization, to begin the process of implementing TQM. The inventory is also useful for educating managers and teams about TQM, in seminars and workshops. And, because it is based on sound theory and careful research, the optical-scan form of the *TQM Assessment Inventory* can be used as a TQM tool, to gather data for organizational assessment and improvement.

The inventory parallels the concepts presented in *Putting Total Quality Management to Work.* The first scale measures the extent to which *TQM tools and techniques* are being used in the organization. Next, five scales assess the extent to which customer concern is built into each of the five quality checkpoints, yielding a score for each QC and an overall *TQM customer quality* score. Finally, a set of eight scales measure the degree to which each of the eight *TQM culture elements* is present in the organization's culture.

Graphic displays of individual and of group or organizational scores help make more concrete and meaningful the concepts presented in the book. The *TQM Assessment Inventory* booklet contains extensive interpretive information, providing a brief, focused summary of the book's key points.

A **Trainer Guide** provides both technical information on the inventory and extensive help for the consultant or group facilitator, including detailed seminar and workshop design plans.

*TQM Assessment Inventory:* $7.95; quantity discounts available.
*TQMAI* **Trainer Guide:** $15.00.